UNTIL THE BIRDS CHIRP: Reflections On The Sixties

MARC A. CATONE

Also by Marc A. Catone

As I Write This Letter: An American Generation Remembers The Beatles
The Giant's Chair

Portions of this book have appeared previously in Beatlefan magazine. Thank you to Bill King, Editor of Beatlefan, for his permission to use herein. Visit http://www.beatlefan.com

DEDICATION

This book is dedicated to the memory of Kevin Javillonar, 1950 – 2013, my friend and classmate, who was a Rock drummer, Tennis Pro, and most of all, a dedicated high school English teacher, loved by his students for over three decades. Witty, humorous, kind and generous, Kevin truly exemplified the Sixties Generation.

Contents

INTRODUCTION

"If you remember the Sixties, you weren't there."

So goes the familiar quote...except it's not true.

There are millions of people who remember the Sixties.

I'm one of them.

When my daughter, Amanda, was a high school student in the early 2000s, I looked inside her United States history book to see what was written about the time period when I was a teenager, the Sixties. The text consisted of three pages. JFK was killed, some folks didn't like the Vietnam War, a couple of men walked on the moon, and a bunch of hippies went to Woodstock and slid in the mud. Three pages...that was it. There was no insight about the most important decade in 20th century America. There was no discussion about the significance the Sixties held for an entire generation of young people. Nothing.

I shouldn't have been surprised by the lack of information in the book. Negative revisionism about the Sixties began during the late 1970s and early 1980s when major corporations bought up most of the print and broadcast media. Ironically, people who hated the progressive movements were now in charge of reporting its history. Despite those reactionary efforts, the Sixties continue to be a current topic in the media, but not on an authentic level. Most discussions are not honest conversations from the people who were influenced by those times. Instead, TV portrays the Sixties as an arcane period when kids had to "get it out of their system" before they became adults. An entire era has been reduced to a stereotypical sitcom plot in which young people find their elders' love beads and bell bottoms in the attic. Everyone has a big laugh over the clothes while ignoring the values of the people who wore them.

Occasionally, TV will offer a special or movie featuring a Sixties theme, but the intent is to make money from musical soundtracks or nostalgic product placements rather than an in-depth look at the times and the thoughts of those who lived it. Even PBS, a network that boasts an unbiased approach to news stories, features more people highly critical of the various Sixties movements than those who view the decade favorably. Their recent documentary on Kent State gave an inordinate amount of time to Pat Buchanan, a notorious ultra conservative, bigot and former speech writer for Richard Nixon. The PBS program ended with a gloating Buchanan spinning his wrongheaded views about Kent State and the anti-war movement.

Often, books about the subject are compendiums by historians or journalists too old (or too young) to have been children of the Sixties. Even in the 21st Century, reports of what happened to people in the Sixties are seldom from those who experienced it in real time.

Many of us, who comprise the Sixties Generation, transferred our idealism into workable solutions and lifestyles as adults. Unfortunately, some of us put our dreams on hold, convinced by corporate naysayers and rightwing talking heads that the accomplishments of the Sixties were a lie. However, something has happened within my age group. Based on conversations with others from my generation, I sense a longing for the spirit of the Sixties. This desire isn't merely the sentimental memory of childhood which affects each generation as it ages. What happened to young people in the Sixties was over and above the normal rebelliousness of youth, beyond the usual search for identity and more important than just being hip. The torch of the Sixties may have flickered over the years, but the fire was never extinguished.

I am part of the Sixties Generation, who experienced a political and cultural decade that began in the early 1960s and ended in the early 1970s. There were many influences absorbed by young people growing up in Sixties America. Not only did a hot house of ideas, attitudes, and trends shape my generation's outlook and values, but we had a lot of fun too. We wanted to discover an alternative to the Protestant Work Ethic. We knew there had to be more than a gift of a gold watch at age 65.

Intuitively, I knew that the Sixties were important as they happened. I felt a responsibility to chronicle events, both big and small, and how they affected me. In the beginning, my recollections were words written down in a diary, a short story for a high school English class or letters to friends. I was able to associate certain episodes and occurrences, what people said and when they said it, with great accuracy. When I reached adulthood there were friends, relatives, and coworkers who relied on my ability to remember.

For many years, I've wanted to put all those childhood, teenage and young adult memories in one place. "Until The Birds Chirp" is a snapshot of my youth from the mid-1950s through the mid-1970s. All of the chapters reveal the impact of events and societal changes, both personal and political, on my formative years with a heavy emphasis on the most important decade of all, the Sixties. The chapters of this book contain joy, sadness, triumph and failure. What they don't contain is apology or regret. There's no room for negativity within the experiences lived and the lessons learned during that decade.

No reporter or pundit is going to talk about the Sixties Generation as accurately as the folks who were there and breathed the air...the people who lived it. No matter what kind of people we've become as adults, the influence of that era was widespread. My life is one story out of millions weaved into the tapestry of the Sixties experience. I hope that other members of the Sixties Generation will be encouraged by my book to tell their histories as well.

If we don't...no one else will.

CHAPTER ONE---What's Up With The Title?

Have you ever read a book with the explanation of its title buried in the middle chapters or never mentioned until the last few pages? This book isn't one of them. I'm going to tell you the meaning of "Until The Birds Chirp" right now. So pay attention...there might be a Pop Quiz later on.

I spent a large part of my life during the Sixties listening to FM Rock radio. Most of the stations were from New York City, their signal strong and loud at my home in Danbury Connecticut. The format was called "free-form." The disc jockeys had the freedom to spin music without adhering to a strict playlist. They played what they wanted to play with little interference from the station manager. Often, the results were a group of songs with similar themes. Other times one song blended into another. Occasionally, the jocks initiated an abrupt change from heavy Rock to Folk ballad. Once in awhile they included a jazz or classical interlude. Unlike their AM radio counterparts, FM Rock disc jockeys didn't speak over or curtail the songs they played. Rock songs were becoming more intricate with long beginnings and climactic endings. Listeners wanted to hear all of the music from the first note to the last.

In early 1971, my favorite album was "Layla and Other Assorted Love Songs" by Derek and The Dominos. The band was a super group formed by Eric Clapton, Duane Allman, Carl Radle, Bobby Whitlock, and Jim Gordon. I knew Clapton from his stints with the Yardbirds, Cream and Blind Faith,

1

Allman from the Allman Brothers, and the other players as superb session men who had recorded or toured with Joe Cocker, Delaney and Bonnie and George Harrison. There were many dynamic songs from the album that stood well on their own merits..."Bell Bottom Blues", "Anyday", "Why Does Love Got To Be So Sad?", and "Have You Ever Loved A Woman?" However, my favorite tune was the title song, "Layla". I listened to it daily on my stereo and heard it many times on FM radio. The passionate vocal by Eric Clapton, the searing guitars of Clapton and Allman, and the pounding piano of Bobby Whitlock found a place in my heart. "Layla" clocked in at just over seven minutes, but I never grew tired of hearing the song from beginning to end.

Then, the years passed and FM radio changed. It was no longer the haven of free-form progressive Rock. Instead, it became a slave to formulaic playlists and omnipresent advertising unwilling to be delayed by the length of a song. One day, I was listening to my car radio when "Layla" came thundering out of the speakers. It had been awhile since I heard the familiar opening riff, so I went with the flow...turning the volume up...really getting into the music. The song was nearing its conclusion, but then something went wrong. The disc jockey talked over the ending. He didn't let the birds chirp.

At the very end of "Layla" there are birds chirping. It's a well-known finish to the classic song. And here was this radio guy cutting it off with inane chatter and a commercial. I was so angry that the tips of my ears turned red. My expectation...damn it...my *right* to hear that song completely from its opening guitar lick to the birds chirping had been violated. As time went by, I began to notice more airplay of

"Layla" with deejays talking over it or starting a new song before its conclusion. The birds were being denied their due.

Simultaneously, by this time in the 1980s, the Culture Wars were in full swing with many of its conservative mouthpieces criticizing the aspirations and accomplishments of the Sixties Generation. Oh, the tales they spun. The truth about what the Sixties meant came under attack by a conglomeration of reactionaries, radical right politicians, fundamentalist Christians, and multi-national corporations. The truncation of "Layla" on the radio was just one more slap in the face from a media coming under the control of owners whose politics demanded the suppression of freedom instead of its encouragement. Music had been our inspiration, muse, and companion. The mutilation of "Layla" was a symbolic trashing of the Sixties spirit.

Social justice, equality, and tolerance were among the many precepts embraced by teens and young adults during the Sixties. Over 50 years later, those principles remain firm for many of us. We're getting older, but our passions, beliefs and hopes have not diminished. For the Sixties Generation, "Layla" is always playing in our hearts. We're not done.

It's not over until the birds chirp.

CHAPTER TWO---Putnam Drive

There is a movie running inside my head. It contains numerous intermissions, but no ads for popcorn in the lobby. The film features people, places, songs and events that have occurred during the past sixty years of my life. Sometimes, I'm the main performer and other times I'm merely an observer. There is no script, but on many occasions I've stepped out of character and tried to be someone I'm not. Whenever that's happened, I've suffered both physically and emotionally. Wanting to be the real me, as opposed to an actor, remains a priority. While living in the now is a worthwhile pursuit, remembering the past gives me a better understanding of who I am. It all began a very long time ago.

The sky of my childhood was an intense shade of blue. Summer mornings found me on a swing under a maple tree. When I looked up, I was overwhelmed by the sensation of flying. Puffball clouds punctuated the sky as my legs pumped higher and higher towards the horizon. I was going somewhere, but never wanted to be anywhere...always happy to be in my backyard.

My mind became the stage for the movie. It wasn't about pirates, knights or soldiers. Those were the people I pretended to be when I played with my friends. Instead, the film was an extension of my thoughts, what I felt about different situations, and how others would react to my behavior, opinions and responses to them. Thinking back on it now, I wonder how something so complex could have been swirling inside the head of a boy so young.

I was born in August 1950, smack dab in the middle of the 20th century, to Campbell (Camp) and Martha Catone. We had a small family of four when my sister, Sara, arrived on the scene in April 1952. We were closer emotionally to my mother's side of the family consisting of Grandma Bella and my mother's sister, Aunt Ruth. Although my father's side lived near us, Dad and his mother, Jennie, had a strained relationship due to his broken-home situation growing up (his father, also named Campbell, was 20 years older than Jennie). Martha also came from a family where her parents didn't get along and argued a lot, but Grandma Bella and Grandpa Jack remained married "for the sake of the children" until they divorced in the 1940s. For all their faults and craziness (what person doesn't think their parents are a little crazy?), my parents gave me a secure foundation. I always felt safe living in their household.

My formative years took place in Danbury, Connecticut, the former "Hat City" of the world and supply depot for the Continental Army during the Revolutionary War. In April 1777, Danbury was invaded by British troops who destroyed supplies and burned down homes. Several people were killed. The American forces, led by General Israel Putnam, traveled and camped throughout the forests and farmlands in the southern part of Danbury. One-hundred and seventy-five years later, a housing authority development was built among those rolling foothills of the Berkshire Mountains...on the street where I lived...Putnam Drive.

In 1953, my family moved from Eighth Avenue to Putnam Drive, not far from the border with the town of Bethel. Most of the neighborhood men had been in World War II and afterward they worked in local factories. The women were stay-at-home Moms who gabbed with each other while hanging up wash on their clotheslines. All the kids were close in age. We were pioneers...the first to live on the street.

Putnam Drive was a cul-de-sac with a large circle turn-around at the end. There were eleven houses on the street, each divided into a two-floor duplex. Every home had a front and back yard, though some yards were larger than others. My side of the street was near "the woods" which separated our street from Fairfield Ridge, another city housing development. 5 Putnam Drive was the second house on the right. The backyard was bordered by a private residence. A white wooden fence separated our two realities...renter from homeowner.

The Najamy family lived next to us in the first house on the street. My earliest memory is of Gilberte "Bunny" Najamy's new-born sister, "Sarah", coming home from the Danbury Hospital in July 1954. My mother took care of Bunny when Fred Najamy drove to the hospital to pick up his wife and baby. I remember Fred's car pulling into their driveway. We ran over to see Bunny's mother, Gil, emerge from the car with little Sarah wrapped in a blanket. Prior to Sarah Najamy's birth, my memories were short, hazy, black-and-white scenes of little consequence, but starting on that summer day in 1954, I began to remember in color on a daily basis. The movie in my head was whirring in earnest.

One year later, in August 1955, my parents threw a large 5th birthday party for me in the back yard. The highlights of that day are captured in an old home movie. It's the first filmed event of my life that I recall in real time. The theme of the party was "Davy Crockett" from the then popular Walt Disney movie. Davy and his gun named "Old Betsy" were figurines on top of my birthday cake. All the kids in the neighborhood, my cousins, grandmothers, and parents participated in the lighting of the candles. They sang "Happy Birthday" while I covered my ears. Bashful was I at all the attention. A spirited game of "Pin the Tail on the Donkey" followed the eating of the cake. There's a scene in the home movie of my mother brushing back my hair with her hand. She's bending over me saying, "You're getting to be a big boy...this is your big day." There's no audio track on the film, but I remember her saying that to me as if it were yesterday.

My best friend on Putnam Drive was Jerry Lefebvre, who lived in a brown house one up from mine. Jerry was a year older than me. He was fearless in all his endeavors and often got into trouble because of them. I followed his lead much to the consternation of my mother, who was quite protective of me. Jerry's backyard was the envy of all the neighborhood kids because the path to "the woods" began there. Most of his backyard was a very steep hill. It was devoid of trees and brush for about 25 feet until the woods began with a wide path of grass wending its way to the hill top. The entire hill, from top to bottom, was more than 100 feet in length.

During the winter, everyone took to Lefebvre's hill with their sleds. In good snow conditions we glided down its full length until our sleds came to a screeching halt on the blacktop of Jerry's driveway. If Jerry's father hadn't shoveled, we continued past the driveway down a smaller slope and then onto the snow covered sidewalk. We whizzed past the front of my house to the entrance of Putnam Drive and stopped just short of Coalpit Hill Road. Considering the amount of traffic, sledding at top speed to the end of the street was quite dangerous, but we didn't think anything bad could happen to us. It was fun and that's what mattered.

Jerry had two younger brothers, Paul and John. All three Lefebvre boys were a handful for their patient mother, Rosemarie. Often, Mrs. Lefebvre's three sons would stray from home. Most times, they could be found playing in a neighbor's backyard or up the hill in the woods. One of my favorite childhood memories is Rosemarie Lefebvre's remarkable "call." Whenever she wanted to summon her children home, she stood on the back or front porch and made the "call." Although quite loud, it was not a yell or a scream...the "call" was pure neighborhood opera. She sang her sons' names. Her song was always in the same order and cadence. She sang Jerry's name first, then expanded Paul's and John's names into two syllables, accenting the second and pausing for the same interval between each boy's name. Rosemarie's melodious tune was unmistakable. I'll bet that anyone who lived on Putnam Drive can still remember her calling the boys home. I like to think there is a remnant of its echo still bouncing among the trees in Jerry's backyard.

As my friends and I grew older, we ventured into the "fields", located beyond the edge of the woods at the top of Lefebvre's hill. The fields were a wide open prairie-like area bordered by Fairfield Ridge at the north edge and Dolan's Sand Banks at the south end. We didn't play with the kids from Fairfield Ridge very often. The "Ridge Kids" were rumored to be stronger and meaner than us. Occasionally, there was a turf skirmish between the two factions, usually broken up by someone's older brother...or his old man. I don't recall any casualties, but those Ridge Kids were tough.

When one entered the fields there was an instant feeling of being in another world, cut off from civilization and parental authority. Just like Peter Pan's "Lost Boys", the Lefebvres, Esposito brothers (Mike and Danny) and I reveled in our freedom as we built forts, had fart contests, and talked about what we were going to do next. Occasionally, we would employ the use of general science in our endeavors. Among our largely unwashed ranks was a boy who could have been a candidate for Don Herbert's "Mr. Wizard" TV show. His name was Ken Stoorza, but everyone called him "Chipper." Ken and I shared the same month and day of birth, except that he was three years older than me. One day, we rigged up a large wooden crate in the woods near the entrance to the fields. Chipper showed up with a large dry cell, some wires and a small light bulb. He placed the light inside the crate and wired it to come on when someone entered the opening. We all stood around waiting to test it. When it worked, we emitted a loud cheer similar to NASA workers upon a successful lift-off. We considered Ken an ingenious lad, years ahead of us all in intelligence and knowledge.

As neighborhood kids came and went, my relationship with the fields changed. I stopped digging foxholes, making mud pies, and smoking an occasional cigarette (stolen from my aunt's purse). Sometime around age 12 or 13, the fields became my sanctuary and eventually my confidante. I communed silently with the fields. I went there to think about different things...school, girls, war, peace, and what it would be like to be an adult. I'd be gone for a couple of hours as I walked and stopped at various "thinking places" along the way. I couldn't put my finger on it, but there was a benign presence in the fields. I knew that the fields cared about what was happening in my life even though I didn't understand what was going on at all. It listened and gave solace.

Today, the fields I knew are all gone. Town houses and condominiums now stand where grass, trees and small boys once played undisturbed. The presence of the field dwells in the shadows. Now, it cries out for release to ears that can't hear above the din of steel and glass.

CHAPTER THREE---Elementary

During the late 1950s, children were taught to honor conformist views. Expanding one's mind was not a desirable goal. "Don't rock the boat" was our guiding light. No institution tried harder to make us into cookie-cutter designs than our schools. I wanted to know why we had to follow certain rules, but my teachers weren't prepared to answer. They wanted me to do what I was told.

My elementary school, South Street School, was located less than two miles from my home. Kindergarten was scheduled to begin in September 1955. However, the new building for the kindergarten classrooms was not ready until January 1956. Class began that month. If only all my school years had been a mere six months in length. That would have suited me fine. I never liked being in school. I enjoyed socializing and fooling around with other kids, and I did fairly well academically, but the day-to-day commitment of six hours became rote and tedious. I wanted out.

Although I was only five years old, the thought of going to kindergarten scared me. A sense of dread swept over me when I realized that my mother was going to leave me at a strange place with boys and girls I didn't know. In those days there wasn't any Pre-K and most children did not attend nursery schools. We went straight from mother to school without a safety net in between.

I heard a lot of crying and yelling on my first day in kindergarten...and it wasn't only from the teacher. Amid the mayhem there stood a boy who was oblivious to it all. He played with building blocks and didn't notice the first day jitters of his classmates. Robbie was a very confident five year old, totally unafraid of his new surroundings. Although he was just a little boy, Robbie's maturity level went beyond his chronological age. In later grades, he developed an ability to entertain his classmates by impersonating famous people and cartoon characters, often using his imagination to recite monologues about current events. I recall Robbie, at age 8, doing an amazing imitation of Jonathan Winters, using the same facial expressions and mannerisms of the well known comedian...manic and funny at the same time.

Robbie and I became buddies. We had the same teachers for most of our elementary school grades. Our 1st Grade teacher was a diminutive woman named Miss Waters, a classic "old maid" school teacher. She was a very quiet, yet intense woman. Apparently, when Miss Waters had Civics class in high school, she was absent the day they discussed the separation of church and state. Therefore, she imposed her strict religious beliefs upon her students. She scared the whole class one day with talk of fire and brimstone. Then, one Monday morning, she criticized Elvis Presley after his performance on the Ed Sullivan Show the night before. She said he was immoral because of the way he shook his legs. When one kid chimed in that his older sister liked Elvis, she shot him a dagger-glare to shut him up.

Today, we hear people complain about prayer not being an organized practice in school. They think there is a conspiracy against the singing of religious songs during Christmas season, claiming that someone has "stolen" Christmas from them. What they forget, or never knew, is that back in the late 50s and early 60s, religious Christmas songs were mandatory for all students in public schools regardless if one were a Christian or not. Eventually, the Sixties Generation's tolerance and advocacy for diversity changed those practices towards a more equitable treatment for all religions during their Holiday seasons.

What I didn't like about 1st Grade was the length of time one had to spend there. In kindergarten, there had been two sessions, morning and afternoon. I went in the morning and was done by lunch time. In 1st Grade, there were half-day sessions for the first couple of weeks, but then we started to go all day. I hated it. During a particular time of stress in my household (Dad was hospitalized for awhile), I balked at going to school and missed a few days. My mother was angry and at her wits' end about it. One day, she took me to school and marched to the principal's office where a discussion about what-to-do-about-Marc occurred. My only recollection is the outcome...I kicked the principal in the shins and ran out the door.

As time went on, I grew accustomed to the length of the school day, but during all of my school years, even in high school, I always had a high rate of absenteeism. Most days off were due to my sinus and asthma problems, but some of my absences, particularly in the higher grades, were because I didn't want to go. I thought of school as a waste of time. There was always something better to do.

Miss Keane was my 2nd Grade teacher. Miss Waters and Miss Keane wanted to do something other than be wives and stay home, but women didn't have many options available to them in the early part of the 20th century. They either became secretaries or went to school to become teachers. However,

Miss Keane was quite different than Miss Waters. She was bold and assertive.

When one is young all adults look old, and if they happen to have gray or white hair, they are ancient. Miss Keane's hair was all-white and she looked to be over 60 years old, but she was probably ten years younger than that. She was...to borrow a rarely used expression these days...a tough old broad. Beneath her granite exterior she was kind and very patient towards me. She also saved me from a killer bee.

One spring day, an errant bee flew in through the classroom window. Unbeknownst to me, it crawled on the inside of my shirt collar and decided to seek out the flesh of my neck. When I realized what was going on, I reached into my shirt and flicked the bee away. However, the bee stung me on both the neck and right hand. I cried out in pain. The bee was on the floor near my desk when I saw Miss Keane's big black high heel squish it into the next world. "That's one bee that will never bother anyone again," she said. And without missing a beat, she returned to her lesson plan.

My buddy, Robbie, was a classmate in Miss Keane's 2nd Grade room. He kept us laughing. School children needed all the humor they could get in the late 1950s. The paranoia of that era had a chilling effect on kids in the United States. We lived in a country fast becoming Fortress America, engaging in a "cold" war against the USSR and teaching its young people to despise and consider with suspicion anything Russian. Everything the United States did was good. Everything Russia did was bad. It was black-and-white with no gradations of color in between. Years later, we realized that our country was the principal instigator of an arms race that had the decimation of the Soviet economy as its primary objective. It "only" took 40 years of covert activity, bloody wars in Third World countries, and the increased power and wealth of corporate America at the expense of the poor and middle classes...but hey...WE WON...didn't we?

During the 50s, all schools were required to conduct H-bomb drills to prepare students for a possible Soviet nuclear attack on the United States. We lined up in the school corridors with our backs against the wall while our instructors ordered us to be silent and not stand near any windows. Looking us straight in the eyes, our teachers explained that if an atomic bomb exploded outside, anyone standing near a window might be cut by broken glass. During one of those bomb drills, as we stood in silence, afraid to look anywhere except straight ahead, Robbie whispered in my ear, "It doesn't matter where we stand. If an H-bomb blows up outside, we'll all be burnt to a crisp." This was a major revelation for me. I didn't understand about the full destructive power of nuclear weapons until that moment. It became clear to me, at age 7, that it was useless to protect oneself against atomic weaponry. There was no place to hide.

I couldn't understand why our country and Russia would want to bomb each other when both nations knew it would lead to the annihilation of the human race. What was the purpose? It defied common sense to be growing up in a world planning mass suicide. It wasn't right for children to worry about being "burnt to a crisp." Every night, I prayed for God to prevent nuclear war.

School, during those early formative grades, wasn't entirely bleak. My favorite memory of Elementary school life occurred then. One afternoon, we were told that something fun was going to happen in our combination gym-auditorium-cafeteria the next day. We weren't given a lot of information about what was going to occur, except for one strange instruction... tomorrow those children who owned "mouse-ears" should bring them to school.

"Mouse-ears" were the hats worn by the Mouseketeers who appeared on the TV show, "The Mickey Mouse Club", which most of us watched daily when we arrived home from school. Being so advised, I arrived at school the next day replete with my Mouseketeer beanie. The teachers led our class into the assembly. Shortly after taking our seats, we all stared towards the stage. There, direct from California, stood a man whose face shined across our TV screens every afternoon. Our special guest was Jimmie Dodd, Mooseketeer and host of the "Mickey Mouse Club."

To this day, I don't know why Jimmie Dodd appeared at my school. I have a vague recollection that he was associated with a charity event occurring in Danbury that week. How South Street School managed to arrange his performance remains an unsolved mystery. But there he was, red hair, freckles, and guitar in hand, wearing his "mouse-ears" and Mickey Mouse Club shirt. He sang a few songs and spoke about the various Mouseketeers we knew and loved.

As the show drew to a close, he requested that all of the kids who had mouse-ear hats to come up on stage with him. My lasting image of that special day is of me, Mouseketeer ears on my head, standing right next to Jimmie Dodd as we all sang the closing song from the "Mickey Mouse Club Show". It was the first time that I participated in a group event with my peers from the Sixties Generation. Sing it with me now, brothers and sisters:

Now it's time to say good-bye to all our company.

M-I-C....see you real soon.

K-E-Y....Why, because we like you.

M-O-U-S-E.

CHAPTER FOUR---Are You Going To Danbury Fair?

Every October, the Danbury schools were closed for one day. Each child received a free ticket to attend Connecticut's "greatest show on Earth", **The Great Danbury State Fair**.

The Fair existed for more than 100 years. It began as an agricultural showcase in the early 1800s and continued as a regularly scheduled event in 1869. As the years went by, during good times and bad (including a major fire), it evolved into something more, greatly aided by the vision and leadership of Danbury's premier showman, John W. Leahy. Mr. Leahy became the major owner of the Danbury Fair during the immediate post-World War II era and brought in new ideas and innovations. The Great Danbury State Fair was a circus, Wild West show, agricultural exhibit, theme park, carnival, and race track all rolled up into one. Located on 100 acres in the southwestern corner of the city, not far from the state border with New York, the Fair drew crowds numbering in the 100,000's for 10 days in October from all over the East Coast.

There was the Big Top where farmers displayed vegetables and fruits for blue ribbons; Gold Town, an Old West replica of Dodge City with saloons, good guys, and outlaws; the New England Village featuring a one-room school house and old country store; dozens of permanent buildings housing pigs, cows, horses(including the Budweiser Clydesdales), assorted poultry, and various home improvements; the Dutch Village, a New Amsterdam era New

York with windmills and other amenities from that time period; a giant Mid-Way with carnival rides, arcades, side shows, and Hoochie Koochie girls; auto-racing daredevils on the racetrack near the Grandstand; huge towering fiberglass figurines of Paul Bunyan and Farmer John; a Pirate's Cove, Cinderella-land, and musical performers; dozens of food vendors serving hot dogs, hamburgers, French fries, pizza, sausage and meatball grinders(subs), Bavarian waffles, cotton candy, candy apples, snow cones, and full-course restaurants; and last, but certainly not least, the daily Fair Parade headed by John Leahy himself.

The night before Fair Day was like Christmas Eve, each child so excited that sleep was nearly impossible. My sister, Sara, and I were no exceptions, dreaming about riding the "Tilt-a-Whirl", playing in the Fort at the Dutch Village, and smacking our lips just thinking about "Jack's French Fries" and the meatball grinders sold at the VFW booth.

I attended the Danbury Fair from about age 3 until age 24, approximately 20 years. The only one I missed during that time period was the Centennial year of 1969. That omission was due to my involvement in college with the Vietnam Moratorium. The last year I went to the Fair was in 1974, right before my wife, Donna, and I moved to Arizona.

The Great Danbury State Fair was part of my heritage. I had the unique experience of seeing it from a different perspective than the average Fair attendee. In 1965, my father, Camp, began working for John Leahy's fuel oil company. He was employed there for about three years. Dad worked for Leahy's fuel oil business during the winter and as part of the Danbury Fair paint and labor crew from spring through fall, including the 10-day run of the Fair in October. The Fair was immense with many permanent buildings and displays that took the crew six months to re-paint, fix, and maintain from the ravages of winter weather.

In 1965, my family had one car. My mother, Martha, got done with her workday before Dad did. Often, I accompanied her on late summer afternoons when she drove to the Fair Grounds to pick him up. It was a thrill to ride through the gates and drive to the paint building, located near the pond in the New England Village. However, it was an eerie experience as well. All of the temporary tents from Fair week were not there. One could look across the flat expanse and see the Grand Stand and Big Top as if they were a stone's throw away. It was hard to imagine that during the run of the Fair it took an hour or more to walk that same area... so thick was the area with people, tents, and food vendors. While we waited for Dad to finish work, I wandered around the Fair. I felt like the last person on Earth walking around all those empty acres. And yet, I treated those hallowed grounds with a reverence that only a Danbury kid could know.

In 1972, I had the opportunity to work at the Fair. My next door neighbor, Fred Najamy, ran one of the few sit-down restaurants, "Freddie's Country Kitchen." His daughter and my good friend, Gilberte, ran the breakfast part of the restaurant called "Bunny's Ham 'n' Egger." Fred was a caterer by profession, but his real money maker was the restaurant at the Fair. That summer, out of college without a job, I worked with Gilberte at a few clam bakes. When she asked me if I wanted to work at her breakfast place at the Fair, I jumped at the chance.

It was a very hard job...up each morning at about 4 AM, on the job by 5:00, and ready to serve breakfast by 6:00 to many Fair workers, carnies and other participants. Gilberte served breakfast all day, although morning was the busiest. At night we put food away, cleaned up, and performed other duties, not getting done until about 10:00. However, I was only 22 years old and had the stamina to do it all.

It was quite a different view of the Fair when one worked there. There were so many people walking by and stopping in during the day. Many from far away, who had never been to the Fair. You wanted to do well. It was a matter of pride to give them good service and make a great impression. There were moments of tediousness and boredom, but I never tired of the Fair whether I was an attendee, son of a Fair worker, or employee. The Danbury Fair was in my blood.

And then came 1981...and it all came to an end. John Leahy died in 1975, and the Fair began to decline financially. Living in upstate New York, I didn't make it to the last year of the Danbury Fair. I don't know all the reasons why the Fair ended. Maybe, it was just the time period, the 1980s...there were new forms of entertainment and distractions, or perhaps with Leahy no longer in charge there was a lack of leadership. Along came a major developer who dangled the right sum of money in front of the eyes of those who had controlling interests in the Danbury Fair, and it was gone...forever. Knocked down, torn apart, never to hear the squeals of delight from children again. In its place, the Danbury Fair Mall was constructed. Just what the world needed...another mall...the 20th century's edifice to planned consumerism.

Fast forward to 1997. My family and I were making an infrequent trip to Connecticut which took us through Danbury. We exited off I-84 to drive around and look at my old neighborhood. We decided to drive down Mountainville

Avenue, which was on the other side of Rogers Park from where I grew up on Putnam Drive. I was driving when my wife told me to stop and turn around. She noticed a house with a lot of things on the front lawn....items from the Danbury Fair.

We pulled into the driveway and marveled at what we saw...old figurines from Gold Town, parts of familiar signs and pieces of buildings from the Fair, and a large bulletin board with dozens of family photos from the Fair. We knocked on the door of the house. An older man answered. His name was Walter Dunlap. We spoke excitedly about our Fair memories and people we knew in common from years ago in Danbury. A chance drive-by became an hour long reminiscence of the Danbury Fair.

Mr. Dunlap had been a State Policeman, who worked the gates, parking lot, and security at the Danbury Fair for many years. When the Fair closed down, there was a major auction of thousands of Danbury Fair items. Many were bought by people representing other Fairs and carnivals across the country, but some were bought by average citizens like Walter Dunlap. However, he didn't buy them to make money. Instead, he displayed the artifacts annually as a tribute to the late Great Danbury Fair during the same week in October that the Fair had run. It was my good fortune to be there during that week in 1997 and see his homage to days past.

Every year, Dunlap began his weekly Fair tribute by visiting the grave of John Leahy, saying a few words there, and leaving flowers. He had known Leahy on a first name basis and spoke of him with great respect

"You know what I miss most about the Fair?" Mr. Dunlap asked me, his eyes wide and bright, "All the wonderful smells."

Instantly, I understood what he meant. He wasn't referring only to the typical food and carnival smells. No, at the Danbury Fair there was an air of conviviality...a liveliness. Every October, the Fair became a large happy organism, and all the attendees, vendors, and entertainers contributed their joy to its existence.

To this day, there are legions of "Walter Dunlaps" who savor the Fair and keep its memory alive in their hearts.

CHAPTER FIVE---Like Wow...Good Buddy

Adults appeared unhappy to me when I was a child. They hated their jobs, bemoaned their finances and complained about aches and pains. They had to pay mortgages and taxes and buy shoes for their kids. It didn't seem to be much fun.

The adult world was obsessed with work. Not just finding a job, but using work as one's main identity in life. Based upon my childhood observations, work was the source of unhappiness and drudgery for the adults I knew. My father, Camp, originally part of the stone mason Catones, withdrew from that work when inner ear problems caused him to be dizzy on the job. He went through a series of occupations. Camp sold swimming pools, vacuum cleaners and for a few years was a shoe store salesman. There were periods of unemployment as well. My mother, Martha, who had been a bookkeeper at an accountant's office before I was born, would work from home for the same firm to make ends meet.

The fathers of my friends and classmates lived in a world of factories where they hated their bosses and barely tolerated the people who worked with them. I couldn't understand why they worked so hard to be so miserable. I knew that I would have to find a job someday. It was not something I wanted to do.

Comic book super-heroes didn't worry about those things. They could lift locomotives, use heat vision, be invisible and most of them could fly. They performed their deeds for free, took off when things calmed down and had secret identities that no one knew. From the age of 7 until around age 13, I was an avid reader of DC comics...Superman, Batman, Flash, Green Lantern and the Justice League of America. I read every issue for about seven years, including the spin-off adventures of Superboy, Jimmy Olsen, Lois Lane and the World's Finest (featuring both Superman and Batman together). When I was in 4th and 5th grades, two boys in my class, Jimmy O'Shea and Mike Baran, shared my love for super-heroes. Upon dismissal, we would often race to the Rogers Park Pharmacy, a short distance from South Street School, to peruse the comic book rack for new issues.

Authority figures felt that the story line and drawings of comic books were below the level of most literature and would lead to one thing...juvenile delinquency. No amount of lectures or warnings deterred me from reading comic books, but on one occasion I had to fight the urge to steal a hubcap after reading about the criminal activities of Lex Luthor. Comic books featuring super-heroes captured my imagination like nothing else before. Classic tales of good vs. evil, colorful villains and an occasional puerile concept of a love story (I thought Lana Lang was hot) filled the pages. They inspired me to write my first short story at age 9. It was a Sci-Fi tale about a planet called "Mica". My buddies, Jimmy and Mike, were the main characters.

One Friday afternoon after school, I convinced myself that I could fly just like Superman. I thought that by jumping from a height, I would take flight. On a practical level, I knew flying was impossible, but I psyched myself into it. Fortunately, I knew that jumping off a roof was dangerous...having read in a newspaper that some kid had died that way. So, early on Saturday morning, I walked to the top of a hill not far from the fields in which I played. There was a large boulder there. I chose that to be my point of lift-off. I took a deep breath, stretched my arms in front of me like Superman and jumped as high as I could into the air...then came crashing down on the hard earth below. I knew from the start that failure would be likely, but in my mind it was all about the attempt.

Around the peak of my comic book reading days, circa 1959, a TV show appeared that suggested there was more to life than being born, going to work and dying. It was called "The Many Loves of Dobie Gillis", but my 4th grade friends and I referred to it as just plain "Dobie Gillis". We watched it every Tuesday night and spent most of Wednesday discussing it during lunch and recess. It was a show about a teenage boy, his friends, family and the girls he liked. Unlike "The Adventures of Ozzie and Harriet", "Father Knows Best", and "Leave It To Beaver", the Dobie character, played by Dwayne Hickman, was an anti-hero, who realized his weaknesses, chided himself with self-deprecating humor, but never gave up in his pursuit to find the perfect girl. Dobie lived in a slightly dysfunctional family. The Gillis household wasn't as warped as the cartoon-like Bundys from the 80s TV show, "Married With Children", but they were an irreverent bunch with just the right amount of foibles to make them seem real.

Although Dobie was the star of the show, my favorite cast member was his "good buddy", Maynard G. Krebs. Looking back on the program from the vantage point of the 21st Century, one can see that Krebs was a stereotype, but for its time his character was thinking outside the box. Maynard, played by Bob Denver, was an amalgam of Beatnik and Bohemian. He wore faded pants, baggy sweatshirts, a scraggly goatee and listened to jazz. Towards the end of the series, his concern with various social causes made him a precursor to late 60s hippies. However, it was his live-for-today-don't-worry-be-happy attitude that earned my respect. For Maynard, work was a road block to a happy life. It didn't matter to me that the Krebs character was a generalization made to depict beatniks as lazy. On the contrary, I saw him as someone who had his priorities straight...to be happy. I didn't know Jack Kerouac or Allan Ginsburg. Instead, Maynard G. Krebs became my introduction to being unconventional, against authority and anti-establishment. The joyful spirit of Maynard made me question all the adult preoccupation with work.

I was in Miss Fleming's 4th grade class during the first season of "Dobie Gillis". She was a vibrant red haired woman, who stood in front of the class and gave a performance regardless of the subject at hand. She spoke dramatically and scolded talkative girls with the admonition, "And who do you think you are, Lady Jane?" Miss Fleming was totally absorbed, yet not self-conscious. One of her quirks was to give a posture award medal at the end of each school day to the deserving student who had exhibited good form sitting at his/her desk (I received it twice, deliberately sitting as straight as I could on a Friday, so I could keep the medal over the weekend and show it to all my friends in the neighborhood).

I did well in History while in the 4th grade and ate up everything Julia Fleming had to offer about Christopher Columbus and the New World explorers. When my parents met with her during an "open house" night, Miss Fleming announced that I was "college material." Mom and Dad were quite proud about this proclamation of academic potential for their son. No one in my father's family had attended college. From that day forward, college became my parents' goal for me, and unwittingly or otherwise, it became my objective as well.

One day during recess in the school yard, Miss Fleming overheard me tell my classmates that I wanted to grow up to be a beatnik, just like Maynard G. Krebs. I can still visualize the harsh glare of disapproval she gave me. Other boys wanted to be cowboys or firemen, but not that Catone kid...a beatnik no less.

At that age, I really had no idea what I wanted to be when I "grew up." However, there was one thing I didn't want to be...a soldier. Joining the army and going to war made absolutely no sense to me. It seemed cruel to go to school, prepare for life, get a job, fall in love and then be killed in a war. Also, I couldn't imagine killing anyone.

I credit my grandmother, Bella, for providing my first insight into the futility and insanity of war. She didn't subscribe to any political ideology, but always voted for Democratic candidates. She was a great admirer of FDR and cried when Roosevelt died in 1945, "He stood up for the little guy," she said. Grandma Bella was a very practical woman. Her brother had been in the trenches of World War One and she was grateful he had survived. Her antiwar stance was quite simple...she didn't want the people she loved to get killed.   She saw the necessity of stopping Hitler in World War II, but couldn't understand the reason for American boys fighting and dying in Korea. One night in the early 1960s, as Grandma and I watched the evening news, there was a report that U.S. military advisers were being sent to Vietnam. Grandma Bella took off her glasses, looked at me and said with anger in her voice,

"Why do we always have to get involved with these damn little countries?"

CHAPTER SIX---1960

1960...no wait...**1960**...just another second...**1960**...that's better, it was a big year.

In December 1959, newspapers, radio and TV trumpeted the impending arrival of 1960. People were excited about the new decade to come. Parents, teachers, and children had many expectations about it. And, of course, the folks on Madison Avenue got into the act. I recall a Chevy radio ad with a jingle written in a western/cowboy style...a deep male voice singing over a strummed guitar, "Cars for the 60s...Cars for the 60s." For me, 1960 was the year I became 10 years old.

The year in which one attains 10 years of age is pivotal. You're no longer a little kid and not yet a teenager. You can still get away with sitting on a parent's lap, but you're also expected to act more mature. A series of events during that year kicked my pre-teen years into gear. It was a transformative moment for me... and America too.

1960 was a year of innovation. Color TV became more popular though still on the pricey side. My parents couldn't afford one of those new-fangled TVs with the round screens. On Friday nights, Dad drove my sister, Sara, and me to an appliance store in nearby Bethel as we joined others gazing at "The Flintstones" in color from the TV showroom window. A few months later, we went to my grandmother's house (Dad's mother Jennie) to watch an episode of "Bonanza" on her new color TV. The Cartwrights had kind of an orange/brown skin tone, but what the heck...it was COLOR.

That same year, our local Danbury radio station, WLAD, tried an experiment in stereo broadcasting. I'm not sure that we heard any difference in the sound, but we told each other that we did. It was an "Emperor's New Clothes" moment for the Catone family.

By 1960, there were less unmanned missiles blowing up on the launch pad at Cape Canaveral. America moved closer to sending a man into space. The following year, Alan Sheppard made his sub-orbital flight and became the first American to take-off towards the heavens. Our principal wheeled a TV set into the cafeteria so all of the kids at South Street School could watch history in the making, but the Russians had beaten us in the space race with the first manned flight.

I was in Miss Fleming's 4th grade class when the year began in January, but by the fall of 1960 many changes transpired:

Friends Old and New

My neighborhood was changing. Some of the original families on Putnam Drive were gone. There was a new wave of kids younger than me. However, one thing remained constant...my friendship with Jerry Lefebvre, who lived next door. We were buddies in the truest sense of the word. I don't remember either of us ever getting angry at each other. We played ball in the circle at the end of the street. We rode our bikes together. We hunted for night crawlers and then went fishing the next day at the Rogers Park Pond. However, it all ended shortly before school started in September when his parents bought a house on the North side of town and Jerry moved away from Putnam Drive.

The scene of his departure is forever etched in my mind. I can still close my eyes and see Jerry and his family climbing into their woody station wagon...his father driving them to the circle at the end of our dead end road...and then Jerry waving slowly to me for the last time as they drove by. Everything moved in slow motion. I stood there silently, looking down at the sidewalk, feeling numb and empty. Although I lived on Putnam Drive for another decade or so, the neighborhood was never quite the same after Jerry left.

A couple of months before the Lefebvres moved away, I became friends with Tony Tartaglia, who lived on Seeley Street, a little over a mile from my house. We were close pals from 5th grade through high school. His mother, Josephine, was president of the South Street School PTA, and my mother, Martha, was the secretary for that organization. Our parents became quite close, often enjoying huge Italian meals together (Josephine, what a fantastic cook), which usually took place at the Tartaglia home. Josephine soon became "Auntie Jo", she was a second mother to me. Her husband, also named "Tony", became "Uncle Tony". For many years in a row, particularly during the summer months, Tony's house was my home away from home. We slept in Tony's tent in his back yard, hiked up the hills off of Mountainville Avenue and Southern Boulevard, and bowled duck-pins at the War Memorial building in Rogers Park, the large city park close to Coal Pit Hill Road and my home on Putnam Drive.

In 1960, my parents relaxed their rules on how far away I could ride my bike. I tasted transportation freedom for the first time. When I rode my bike to Tony's house on Seeley Street, on the opposite side of Rogers Park from my home, I traveled across Coal Pit Hill Road, down hilly Overlook Road, and then took the main road through the park. At the corner of South Street and Main Street, I made a left turn past the Rogers Park Pharmacy and then a left onto Mountainville Avenue. Seeley Street was the first street on the right. The following year, I discovered a short-cut through one of the park's ball fields to Mountainville Ave... that saved me a lot of travel time.

Seeley Street had one of the steepest hills in Danbury. Its summit was on Deer Hill Avenue. Riding down Seeley became a challenge for bicyclists. Those were the days before speed-bikes, helmets, and shin pads. Tony, his neighbor and pal, Mark Holmes, and I developed techniques for traveling the distance from top to bottom without suffering a lot of bruises, cuts, and scrapes. Riding down that hill gave me a thrill, accompanied by the fear that I might not be able to stop. One had to know when to start putting on the brakes or else suffer the consequences of bolting into the traffic of Mountainville Avenue at the bottom of the hill. Hitting a stone or losing control of the handlebars could result in a trip to the emergency room...or the morgue.

Baseball:

1960 was the year I began my lifelong love of Major League baseball. Although I was no stranger to the game, I became hooked on our National Pastime that year. My father, Camp, loved baseball as well. I spent many a late Sunday afternoon watching double-headers from Yankee Stadium on our old black-and-white Zenith TV. Dad taught me the rules of the sport along the way. He sat in front of the TV as Mel Allen and Red Barber announced the Yankee games on WPIX-

Channel 11. Dad knew every aspect of the game...sometimes "correcting" the umpires vociferously. He pounded his fist on the arm of the family sofa when something went wrong and clapped his hands when the right play was made. His passion was contagious.

My father didn't like the New York Yankees, but he went to Yankee Stadium with his father (Grandpa Campbell) and watched a World Series game there in the late 1930s. He saw both Gehrig and DiMaggio play. How great that had to be. Dad and Grandpa Campbell also went to Yankee Stadium a few times in the 1950s as well. However, Dad was really a New York Giants fan. His beloved Giants, along with their rivals, the Brooklyn Dodgers, moved to California in 1958 and broke New Yorkers' hearts. Grandpa Campbell also moved to the Golden State in 1960 and joined Dad's brothers, Richard and Kenny, near San Francisco. The Yankees remained as the only team in New York City.

When I asked Dad why he didn't like the Yankees, he replied that they were "getting too big for their britches" and the players took it for granted that they would always be in the World Series every year. Dad grew tired of seeing the Yankees win in almost every year of the 1950s. He wanted someone else to have a chance. Over the years, I also grew to resent the Yankees' assumption of supremacy and dynasty. I must admit that my opinion about the team from the Bronx has not wavered in over 50 years.

In 1960, my parents bought me a baseball glove. It was the first one I ever owned. Dad and I played "catch" almost every night after supper that summer...breaking in the new glove. When I saw my father catch the ball using only his glove hand, I tried, unsuccessfully, to do the same. He said to me, "Beginners use two hands." In a game that often serves as a metaphor for life, that piece of fatherly advice has helped in many situations I've encountered, literally and figuratively.

The World Series of 1960 was the first Fall Classic that I followed from beginning to end. Of course, the Yankees were the American League representatives. This time they faced the National League's Pittsburgh Pirates. I was not familiar with the Pirates until the Series began, but as the games progressed I felt a bond with the Pirate players. They became the team I wanted to see win. By Game # 7 on October 13th, I was a Pirates fan.

In 1960, World Series games were played in the afternoon. The weekday games were well underway by the time I arrived home from school. In Game Seven, the Yankees held the lead until the Pirates' half of the 8th inning when Pittsburgh went ahead. Then, in the top of the 9th, New York tied the game. In the bottom of the 9th inning, Pirates' second baseman, Bill Mazeroski, took his turn at bat before the Pittsburgh crowd.

Every baseball player fantasizes about such a moment with a tie score in the bottom of the 9th in the seventh game of the World Series. "CRACK" went Mazeroski's bat, sending the ball over the outfield wall at Forbes Field in Pittsburgh. HOME RUN, HOME RUN, HOME RUN. The Pirates won the World Series. The entire Catone household was ecstatic.

My mother, who was not given to such outward displays of emotion, actually jumped out of her chair into mid-air and let out a scream (I wish there was a freeze-frame of that). My father was yelling and clapping. I started to whoop it up. We couldn't believe it.   The mighty Yankees lost...the upstart Pirates won.

I've enjoyed many a baseball thrill in my life, but no single play has ever been more sweet to savor...no subsequent hit has contained more jubilation... as when Bill Mazeroski belted that home run to win the 1960 World Series. That day was a ray of hope. For the first time, I realized that underdogs can come out on top, and I learned that powerful institutions, like the New York Yankees, can come tumbling down.

Romance:

In the late summer of 1960, something happened to my heart. I experienced my first "crush."   A full blown kick-out-the-jams CRUSH on a girl who was four years older than me. At age 10, I had fallen for an older woman.

"Sherry" lived on Coalpit Hill Rd across from the entrance to Putnam Drive. I don't remember why, but around August she started visiting my family. In retrospect, she may have been trying to gain the attention of an older boy who lived next door to me, but I was oblivious to that. Almost every day, she was there playing games and reading books with Sara and me. Sometimes, I rode my bike over to Sherry's house and played with her dog, all the while staring at Sherry with longing eyes.

I was infatuated with Sherry and was sure that I was in love with her. Well, I was in love as much as a 10 year old boy could understand. I acted goofy in a show-off way in front of her and pouted when I didn't see her for more than a day. Whether she was aware of my devotion to her, I don't know, but when summer ended she began her freshman year in high school...and I was a kid in 5th grade. My one-sided summer "romance" was over.

Politics:

Sherry's presence had a lasting impact on me in another way. She was a very intelligent and scholarly 14 year old girl. During that month of August, I listened intently as Sherry and my father talked about religion and politics as we sat around our backyard picnic table. They had friendly arguments about her devout Catholicism (Dad was a lapsed Catholic) and about the Senator from Massachusetts, John F. Kennedy, who was the Democratic candidate for president. Kennedy was also a Catholic. There was a lot of controversy about whether a president of his faith would be loyal to the United States or to the Pope in the Vatican. Dad was for Republican candidate Richard Nixon and Sherry wanted Kennedy to win.

Although I had memorized the names of all the presidents in chronological order when I was 7 years old (there were far less presidents to remember then, making it much easier than today), politics was all new to me. 1960 was the first year that I had a keen interest in the outcome of the election. Perhaps, it was because the only president during my early years was Eisenhower. Ike was a grandfather figure to me...he looked and acted old. It hadn't occurred to me that a president could be youthful. And here were two relatively younger men, Kennedy and Nixon, vying to take Eisenhower's place. The spirit of the race captivated me, even though I didn't understand the differences between the two candidates.

At age 10, I wanted my parents' electoral choices to win. Mom and Dad were for Nixon, which meant that I supported him. Being for Nixon was tough on me. There were many Roman Catholic kids in my neighborhood and at school. They and their parents supported Kennedy. I was the lone boy wearing a Nixon button. One of my classmates tore it off my shirt, put a scratch on it, and handed it back to me.

My 5th grade teacher was a man named Joe Kilcran. Not only was Mr. Kilcran my first male teacher, he was also the youngest teacher I ever had. He was only in his mid-20s and fresh from a stint in the Army. You couldn't be more Irish, more Catholic and more of a Kennedy supporter than Kilcran. My classmates and I couldn't help but see the joy in his eyes whenever he spoke to us about John F. Kennedy. When Kennedy won, he was beside himself with happiness. A different kind of politician, with a young wife and children, was about to be president.

Kennedy announced his Cabinet appointments during his time as President-elect. After each announcement, Mr. Kilcran wrote down each Cabinet member's name on the blackboard...Rusk, Ribicoff, McNamara etc. He told the class that we were living at the dawn of a great America with a new group of leaders to guide us. Joe was full of hope. His enthusiasm captivated all of us, including me, the boy who wore the Nixon button. We were excited by the promise of the New Frontier, in which a benevolent United States would promote democracy at home and abroad.

And we, the children of 1960, would be its messengers.

CHAPTER SEVEN---Of Cabbages And Kings

My maternal grandfather, Jack Nacman, died of a heart attack at age 62 in 1959 as he waited for a train in Grand Central Station to take him home to Bethel CT. I was a bit afraid of Grandpa Jack. He was a gruff man who had worked himself up through the garment district of New York and eventually owned a dress factory. He was an uneducated man...never went beyond 5th grade...and a restless sort whose disposition resulted in a "wandering eye", much to the agony of my grandmother, Bella. They divorced before I was born.

While growing up, I heard a lot about his philandering, but I remember him as the person who introduced me to Chinese food, allowed me to push the button for the lunch whistle in his factory and always gave me a shiny quarter when we said our good-byes. But most of all, I associate him with the town of Bethel.

The Danbury-Bethel town line was only a half-mile south from the entrance of my home on Putnam Drive. My grandfather lived about a mile away at the beginning of Greenwood Avenue, just off of Grassy Plain Street and across from the Sycamore Drive-In restaurant. He, and his second wife, Dare, rented one floor of a large old house (previously known as the Blue Cedar Inn) which contained many rooms for kids to run around and play. In the backyard was a big fountain with a basin surrounded in the back by a semi-circle high hedge.

When I was around age 7, the owner sold the old house. The property became the site of a First National supermarket and Friendly's Restaurant. Grandpa Jack moved down

Greenwood Avenue to Elizabeth Street, off of Blackman Avenue. Nearby was Parloa Park, which featured a large playground with two giant slides (one bumpy, the other flat). My sister, Sara, and I spent hours playing there. Bethel was our second home.

Much has been written about the fictional town of "Mayberry" from "The Andy Griffith Show". It was the "down home" feeling about Mayberry that endeared television audiences to the show for many years. They longed to live in a quiet small town where all the businesses were located on Main Street and everyone knew each other by their first name. Bethel was the real Mayberry.

It was a quick trip from Putnam Drive down Fleetwood Ave and across Grassy Plain St to visit my father's favorite hang-out, Scholl & Sons Meat Market. He was friends with the owner, Elwood "Al" Scholl. Most Friday nights, Dad could be found at the meat market, often waiting on customers to help Al when the store was busy (no mystery why we always had the best cuts of meat to eat at home). By the time I was five years old it became a tradition for Al Scholl to cut a slice of bologna for me each time I showed up at his store. He never forgot, even during my infrequent visits as a teenager. "Here, have a slice of bologna," he said with a big smile. I was always surprised that he remembered.

Next door to the meat market was a variety store, Hogan's & Bennett's, where I bought comic books, baseball cards, and sparklers for the 4th of July. About a mile away, just beyond the small and cozy railroad station, was the heart of Bethel on Greenwood Avenue. Within a two block area was Zoel Pellerin's barber shop, Nelson's hardware store, Mullaney's variety store, and the Fountain Restaurant. The local bank, post office, public library, and Bethel High School were across the street

Every two weeks, I visited Zoel's barber shop to get my "ears lowered." Two chairs...no waiting. He let me read comic books while he cut my hair. Afterwards, I went next door to Nelson's Hardware to look at all the gizmos and gadgets displayed in wicker baskets on the hardwood floors.

Further up the hill on Greenwood Avenue was the "Doughboy" memorial park, a tribute to U.S. troops of World War One, circled by other stores and businesses. Across the street from the monument was Noe's clothing store. Every August I went there, dutifully and unhappily, with my mother to buy back-to-school clothes. I had to try on many pairs of pants, and I hated it. To this day, I break into a cold sweat when entering a dressing room. Just beyond Noe's was the Bethel Food Market, one of the first grocery stores to be open on Sundays in defiance of the "blue laws" which called for most stores to be closed on the Sabbath.

Bethel was the true Mayberry. The only things missing were a sheriff without a gun, a deputy with only one bullet and a red-haired kid named Opie riding his bike down the middle of town.

During the early 1960s, my father, Camp, worked as a shoe salesman in various stores in Danbury and the surrounding area. In 1963, Dad opened up his own shoe store on Greenwood Avenue in Bethel. "Camp's Shoe Store" was a tremendous undertaking for the Catones. Finding the right location, signing contracts with shoe manufacturers, Endicott-Johnson and Tingley Rubber Boots, and furnishing the store took a lot of time in the late Summer and early Fall of that year. The whole family helped out, including some financial backing from Grandma Bella and Aunt Ruth (Mom's older sister). Tony Tartaglia Sr. (father of my friend Tony) lent his carpentry skills to the proceedings. Tony Sr. and Dad built the shelves for the shoes. I assisted as best I could. The shoe store was next door to the Fountain Restaurant, not far from Nelson's Hardware, the barber shop and train station. I ran errands to the bank and the post office for my father, and then I'd go to the Fountain restaurant to buy some take-out roast beef sandwiches for lunch. One of the perks for the chores I did.

At the time, I was 13 years old and in 8th grade at Main St School, the largest Junior High School in Danbury. I always thought of Main St School as a prison. We were housed in an antique of a building which contained an overcrowded student body and, with a few exceptions, we were taught by a bunch of lackluster and uncaring teachers. The school had no gym. The cafeteria was located inside an older free-standing house in the middle of the asphalt parking lot playground. On the second floor of the old house was the Art Room. Every day, during both good and bad weather, we trounced our way outside for lunch and art class. To put it bluntly, Main Street School sucked...big time.

Helping my father with the details of the shoe store, assisting customers, and running errands up and down Greenwood Avenue late weekday afternoons and on weekends was a welcome relief to the almost Dickensian surroundings I found myself during the rest of the week at school.

Camp's Shoe Store was in full swing on the Friday before the week of Thanksgiving. I was in 7th period study hall preparing for my 8th period spelling test while daydreaming about the weekend. The study hall teacher looked bored sitting at her desk, frowning at kids who were talking, when all of a sudden another teacher burst through the door and whispered something in her ear. All the color drained from her face. She looked like she was about to collapse. Then the bell rang and we went to our homerooms for the spelling test.

In the hallways of Main Street School there was a low buzz among the students with hushed tone inquiries, "Did you hear?" By the time I reached my homeroom, most of the kids had heard bits and pieces. My teacher, Mr. Caterson, told us all to quiet down. He leaned backwards against the front of his desk; arms crossed, and announced that the rumors were true. Gun shots had been fired at President Kennedy during his trip to Dallas and he was wounded...no other details were available. To this day, I don't remember if we took the spelling test or not. My next memory is the ring of the dismissal bell. We left with the knowledge that the president had been shot, but not much else.

Every day after school, I walked down Main Street to South Street elementary school where my mother's car was waiting to pick up Sara from her 6th grade class. Usually, I was happy on Friday afternoons, leaving school behind for two whole days. But, that day was different...all was quiet. My daily walk seemed to take forever. The one thought racing through my mind was to get home and turn on the TV set. There had to be some news about what was going on. I feared that our nation might be under attack from our mortal enemies, the Soviets. Certainly, they must be the culprits in this shooting. Who else could have done this? Images of World War III, with nuclear bombs exploding, popped into my brain. I had the same helpless what's-gonna-happen-next feeling many years later on a September morning in 2001.   I tried to walk as fast as I could down Main Street, clinging to the hope that JFK's wounds were superficial.

Then the trip became surreal. As I passed by St. Peters School, I looked into the small garden containing a statue of the Virgin Mary.   On their knees were several nuns and school children in a circle around the statue. No words could be heard. All were in silent prayer...oblivious to the world around them.

That's when it hit me. Kennedy must be dead. The rest of my walk consisted of an internal debate, "he must be dead" vs. "he can't be dead".   When I reached my mother's car, I stumbled into the back seat and blurted out, "Did you hear that President Kennedy was shot?"   To which my mother replied the five small words that still echo in my head today,

"The poor man is dead."

It was official.   John F. Kennedy was dead.   The first president to be assassinated since McKinley, over 60 years earlier.   The first American president assassinated in the lifetimes of our parents and some of our grandparents. It was a tragedy uniting all living generations for one terrible moment. A very black Friday on an otherwise sunny day.

Later that afternoon, Mom drove me back downtown to the public library to get a book for a school project. The flag was at half-staff.   The librarians were somber... just going through the motions. As day passed into night, we went to Dad's store. While there, the town drunk of Bethel...their very own "Otis Campbell"...walked by and flashed the front page of a New York City newspaper against the front window of the store. Peering out of the darkness into the brightly lit store, he looked like a specter with the headline:

KENNEDY DEAD

It was a very long day ushering in a weekend full of grief, disbelief, the on-camera murder of the alleged assassin and the Monday funeral with little John-John saluting the coffin of his dead father. All those images remain forever in the minds of those who remember. That one event had a profound impact upon all of our lives, then and now. The assassination was the beginning of America's loss of innocence, an erosion that continues to this day. A few years later we realized there was a shadow government of the United States with its dirty tricks done here and abroad. One can look back at that bleak day in Dallas and say that's when the mask began to slip...that's when a large segment of the American populace began to get wise. And that's why Friday, November 22, 1963 stays with us...it's the first chapter in an unfinished national tale.

A few months after the Kennedy assassination things went from bad to worse for Camp's Shoe Store. The business was losing money. The only other shoe store in Bethel was owned and operated by the same Bethel family for generations. Dad knew he would be up against stiff competition from the beginning. It was hard to crack that market and loyalty. Shortly before my graduation from 8th grade, Dad decided to stop the bleeding and closed the shop.

We dismantled everything we built months earlier. The shelving was broken down, fixtures were taken apart and shoes were boxed up to be mailed back to the distributors. On the final day, I was busy sealing up boxes of shoes. Dad was standing behind the check-out counter. I asked him a question without glancing up from my task at hand. After his reply, I looked straight at him...he didn't sound like my father. I heard the choked sounds of Dad's voice and saw his eyes, red with tears, as he looked quickly away from me and gazed out the window. I had never seen my father cry before. I didn't say anything and continued taping up the box of shoes. At that moment, I understood the sadness about losing the shoe store... the finality of it all. Dad was a few months shy of 40 and his dream on Greenwood Ave was over.

That day, he wasn't just my father, he was also a human being vulnerable to life's disappointments. I loved him. But, I didn't know how to tell him...or if I should.

CHAPTER EIGHT---We're Not In Kansas Anymore

My family watched "The Jack Paar Program" every Friday night on NBC-TV. Paar had been the controversial host of "The Tonight Show" for five years, but on "The Jack Paar Program" NBC gave him more leeway with the direction of the show. Often, his eclectic guests were Zsa Zsa Gabor and Jayne Mansfield, comedian Jonathan Winters, and British humorist Alexander King. I didn't always understand what they were talking about, but there was no other show like it on TV.

On January 3, 1964, I was watching the program when Jack announced that he had a film clip of a Rock 'n' Roll band from England. He prefaced the screening of the film by rolling his eyes, making jokes, and warning us about what we were about to view. Despite his teasing, what I saw that night enthralled me. It was a group of musicians, who called themselves The Beatles, performing a song titled "She Loves You" in front of a live audience. I couldn't believe my eyes and ears. The band consisted of four guys, their shaggy hair combed down above their eyes, singing and playing the most original sounding music I had ever heard in my life.

Their mostly female fans were screaming, swooning, and crying in response to them. It was a wild scene to behold. In retrospect, the videotape was grainy and the sound quality not the best, but that film was my introduction to The Beatles and the mania they created. I was captivated by everything I saw...the young guys with strange haircuts, the screaming girls, but most of all by the music itself. The harmony of the song was sweet, yet discordant. The tune was haunting, yet jubilant. "She Loves You" charmed and mesmerized me. Days later, after hearing it only once, I recalled the tune as if I'd known it for years.

A week or so later, I was riding in the family car with my father. Dad had the radio tuned to the local Danbury station which usually played songs written before the advent of Rock 'n' Roll. As we drove past the Old Oak Restaurant on Liberty Street, the sound of pounding drums and wails of "yeah, yeah, yeah" filled the car. Instantly, I recognized the song as "She Loves You" by that British group I saw on "The Jack Paar Show". I was transfixed by the sound when suddenly the music stopped. Dad turned off the radio.

I pleaded, "Turn it back on, that's The Beatles."

To which he replied, "I don't care who it is, I don't want that junk playing in my car."

In 1964, I was on a path towards being a total nerd (I even carried a briefcase to school). I wasn't familiar with the current music scene. Unbeknownst to me, The Beatles were starting to get a lot of radio airplay in America. Their song, "I Want To Hold Your Hand" was rush-released in America on 12/26/63. Originally, the record was set to come out on 1/13/64, but due to increased demand, Capitol records moved up the release date. "She Loves You", the first million-selling record for The Beatles in England, had been released in the USA during September 1963, but it never reached the Top 100. By mid-January 1964, "I Want To Hold Your Hand" was on its way to being the first Number One song for The Beatles on this side of the pond. The re-released "She Loves You" was close behind.

During the last week of January, I overheard kids in my 8th grade homeroom talking about The Beatles. I found out that the group was coming to America the following week. Excitement was in the air at Main Street Junior High School. Aura Showah, a girl in my homeroom, showed me a teen magazine with a photo of The Beatles in it. Another friend told me where all the New York City Rock and Roll radio stations were on the dial. Soon, Sara and I were listening to WABC, WMCA, and WINS. We were tuned into deejays Cousin Brucie, Scott Muni, Dandy Dan Daniels, Harry Harrison, Murray the K and Mad Daddy.

Listening to those radio stations opened up a whole new world for me. Overnight, I went from "L7" to hip. But best of all, in less than a week, The Beatles were flying from Great Britain to the newly named JFK Airport in New York. They were going to make three consecutive Sunday night appearances on "The Ed Sullivan Show". We couldn't wait.

On Thursday, 2/6/64, Sara (who saw The Beatles before I did...on CBS News in December 1963) bought the Capitol 45 rpm record, "I Want To Hold Your Hand". We listened to it ten times in a row, then flipped it over to hear the "B" side, "I Saw Her Standing There", and played that for just as long. The next day, Friday, February 7th, I bought "She Loves You" at Mullaney's variety store in Bethel. At last, I could listen to the song whenever I wanted. The Beatles landed in New York City that same day.

Performers coming all the way from England to appear on an American TV show were the exception and not the rule in 1964. When their plane landed, The Beatles, welcomed by thousands of screaming fans, were greeted as if they were benevolent alien beings bestowing special gifts upon the Earth. Teenagers and young adults were ready for a new musical direction and experience. The Beatles provided both.

The Fab Four were about the same age as their audience, wrote many of their songs and sang like angels. The totality of The Beatles...their music, appearance, and irreverent humor caused a frenzy among young people not seen before or since.

When the mop-topped lads from Liverpool descended upon the Big Apple, all of the media were in attendance. The weekend of 2/7/64 - 2/9/64 was surrounded by a constant stream of words and photos of The Beatles. They were inescapable. Open up the New York Daily News and there were The Beatles. Turn on the TV and there they were at JFK airport on channels 2, 4, and 7. The press conference at the airport was my introduction to The Beatles' style. They were in command as the TV and newspaper reporters tossed questions at them, answering many tongue-in-cheek. The reporters ate it up. The Beatles were so natural...unlike the wooden teen idols of early 60s America. They didn't take themselves seriously...even if we did.

The next morning, the New York papers contained photos of screaming teenagers gathered outside the Plaza Hotel where The Beatles stayed. Occasionally, one of the four would poke his head out from a window and the noise level in the street below would raise a decibel or two. TV cameras rolled when three of The Beatles took a walk in Central Park. George Harrison was nursing a sore throat and remained in the hotel to recuperate. During their stroll through the park, WNBC-TV Channel 4 reporter, Gabe Pressman, caught up with John, Paul, and Ringo. In a classic moment, Pressman compared Ringo Starr's hairstyle to the caveman figures in the Museum of Natural History across the street. Ringo replied, "I don't like your tie", which was the same line that George

Harrison said to Beatles record producer, George Martin, during their first recording session in 1962.

Sunday night was always a "bath night" in my house. It didn't matter how well I scrubbed myself during the rest of the week...Sunday was the night I had to take a plunge in the tub. Bath night was still on for the evening of February 9, 1964 even though The Beatles would be performing on "The Ed Sullivan Show" in less than an hour. After washing off any remnants of the 1950s, I sat my clean body down on the couch and waited with great anticipation. Ed Sullivan, who always looked like he wore a suit one size too small, talked about how the press corps loved those "youngsters from Liverpool." Then he introduced the band. Paul counted in "1, 2, 3, 4" for "All My Loving" and the youth revolution of the Sixties began in earnest.

In total, The Beatles sang five songs during two separate segments of the hour long program. "All My Loving" came before "Till There Was You", which was followed by "She Loves You." The second set of the evening consisted of "I Saw Her Standing There", and "I Want To Hold Your Hand."

I felt an affinity towards John Lennon beginning with The Beatles' first press conference two days earlier. There was something witty...a bit more clever...about him when he answered questions from the press at JFK airport. Then, I read where he was the only Beatle who was married. Usually, the marriage of a male popular singer was the "kiss of death" career-wise. Many young stars denied being married as a means of keeping a romantic image with their female audience. Lennon's marriage to Cynthia, and his young son, Julian, didn't deter girls from screaming over or proclaiming their "love" for him. It made me think that Beatle John might have an edge on his three band members. He "got away" with a show biz taboo. He was able to be himself...to be genuine. All of The Beatles were real in their own way, but Lennon was a distinct personality from that first visit to America and for years afterwards. At age 13, I was in search of my own identity and John Lennon became a role model for me.

Beatlemania hit American girls hard. Sara, at age 12, was one of them. I have fond memories of her going absolutely crazy every time a Beatles song came on the radio. Later, I would listen in amazement as she and her girlfriends fantasized about marrying one of The Beatles. Each girl was convinced that if one of The Beatles met her, he would fall in love immediately. Early on, I realized that this was a "girl" thing that I could never understand completely. However, I did experience some fun from it all. One day, while using a Liverpudlian accent, I pretended to be Ringo speaking to one of Sara's friends on the telephone. She must have known that the voice on the other end of the line didn't really belong to any of The Beatles, but she went along with the whole routine of crying, screaming, moaning...acting as if she were really talking to Ringo.

Two houses up the street from my home on Putnam Drive lived Nancy Esposito. She was a fervent Beatlemaniac. During the summer of 1964, the soundtrack album from the movie, "A Hard Day's Night", was released. Nancy always reacted the same way upon hearing the song, "Tell Me Why." During the last verse of the song, John and Paul sing the line, "Is there anything I can do?" in falsetto. Every time Nancy heard that lyric, she would let out a loud scream of delight. Very late one August night, I was outdoors on my front porch listening to my transistor radio. "Tell Me Why" came on. The high-pitched line had just been sung when off in the distance I heard a girl's scream pierce the night air. THAT was the power of Beatlemania.

In August 1964, The Beatles' first movie, "A Hard Day's Night", opened at the Palace Theater in Danbury. Sara, our friend Gilberte "Bunny" Najamy, and I arrived at the theater thinking we would be the first ones there. Wrong. Kids were lining up at the theater ticket booth outside. About an hour before the movie started, the crowd began to grow. I heard the first sounds of girls screaming. A half-hour before the doors opened, I felt my body being squeezed against the glass doors of the building. The crowd became noisy as they chanted, "Open the doors." Finally, the doors were unlocked and we spilled into the lobby. We scurried for seats as close to the screen as we could.

The movie started. There were my idols, larger than life on the silver screen, speaking in those strange English accents and singing new songs. However, the noise level of the girls screaming in the audience was so intense that it was impossible to understand what The Beatles were saying. Every close-up of John, Paul, George and Ringo brought fever pitch whoops and yells from the mostly female crowd. I thought to myself...this is what Beatlemania must be like at a concert...and The Beatles aren't even here. Imagine what it would be like to see them in person.

Most people from our parents' and grandparents' generations viewed The Beatles with suspicion and disdain. They were considered nothing more than four indistinguishable mop-tops playing loud music accompanied by unintelligible lyrics. Some considered The Beatles to be a threat to civilization...that the band was part of a communist plot to infiltrate American youth and take over their minds. Many parents and teachers played along with their children's preoccupation with the Fab Four, saying among themselves that it was only a fad...like the hula hoop... and would fade quickly.

I was a pretty mouthy kid among my classmates and friends, but usually quite reticent when it came to speaking up to a teacher. In the spring of 1964, my 8th grade Social Studies teacher told the class that no one would remember who The Beatles were in five years. I reacted with great objection, proclaiming loudly that not only would people remember The Beatles in five years, but everyone would still know who they were in twenty years. I had total confidence in that prediction. My teacher just smiled, most likely thinking I was naïve.

The Beatles have stood the test of time. Over 50 years so far, a fairly impressive accomplishment. They were the real deal. During their career, The Beatles were innovators, inventors, and catalysts, both musically and socially. They gave their original fans the inspiration that group effort can work on many levels. Many ideas that came from the Sixties Generation had their beginning from the path of success of The Beatles. Young people were making changes on their own, defying the old order, and reinventing the world. The Beatles, by example and deed, personified a common Sixties feeling...*Anything was possible*. The Beatles represented the hopes and dreams of millions as the Sixties progressed. They changed...we changed. We grew up with them as they grew up with us.

I've written thousands of words about The Beatles...trying to explain their popularity and what they meant to the world, particularly when they first visited America in February 1964. However, the best description about the significance of The Beatles did not originate with me. It's based upon a popular theory called "The Wizard of Oz" analogy.

Basically, it goes like this. In the movie, "The Wizard of Oz", the film is in black-and-white until Dorothy and her house are dropped by the tornado in the Land of Oz. When Dorothy ventures out the door the film turns into radiant color. Similarly, American culture was a dull black-and-white, but when The Beatles arrived they brought color to the world. For me, and other teenagers, our lives were black-and-white, formulated and predictable, but once The Beatles appeared, a veil lifted showing us new possibilities. Our generation realized that there were other ways of thinking...living...being.

The Beatles provided the spark.

CHAPTER NINE--Satisfaction

The fragmented sound of Gary Lewis singing "This Diamond Ring" bounced off the houses on Putnam Drive as I shoveled heavy wet snow from my sidewalk. Earlier that morning, the fire station horn on Main St sounded the news, NO SCHOOL. Half awake, I fell back asleep with a big grin on my face. No school. No responsibilities. Freedom.

The Rogers Park Pond, less than a half-mile from my home, had been cleared of snow. Skaters were showing up as WABC-AM blared from the loudspeakers on top of the skating hut. Depending on the wind's direction, music reached my house with crystal clarity for several seconds then faded out and rolled back towards Coalpit Hill. The Moody Blues were saying "Go Now" when I finished the driveway. I stood there for awhile taking in the white wintry scene. This was my time. It was good to be young and alive in 1965.

Girls were on my mind. I was "in love" with a different girl every week during my freshman year at the new Danbury High School on Clapboard Ridge Road. However, my libido was all dressed up with no place to go. No matter how cool I considered myself, hair combed down perfectly below the right eyebrow, I was a bundle of shyness and insecurity around the opposite sex. I fantasized about girls during the day and dreamed about them at night, but I felt like Vinnie Barbarino from "Welcome Back Kotter":

"Mr. Kotter, I can't help it...I've got girl-i-tis."

Vinnie always scored on TV, but that didn't happen to me in the real world. I was afraid to initiate conversations with my female peers unless it was about something neutral, like homework or test scores. Just thinking about asking a girl out to the movies gave me a stomach ache. I was a bunch of raging hormones trapped in silence. My brain suggested restraint while thoughts based upon another organ sent a different message.

Society gave teens mixed signals when it came to sex. The patriarchal double standard was still alive and well in 1965. Parents and educators insisted that sex belonged only within the exclusive province of marriage, but TV, radio, and popular entertainment indicated otherwise. Males were expected to prove their manhood by having frequent sex with many women, but they had to marry virgins. To paraphrase Lenny Bruce, every guy was looking for a woman who was both Saturday night hooker and Sunday school teacher.

I was the epitome of sexual naiveté at age 14. I was completely shocked when a classmate reported that he had intercourse...describing his experience in graphic details. I couldn't believe that anyone my age had done such a thing. He was lying most likely or at the very least stretching the truth, but my friends and I were impressed by his story. I was young, gullible, and had never kissed a girl who wasn't related to me. Fortunately the odds were in my favor that I might get a girl to like me. After all, I attended the largest high school in Connecticut with well over 2,000 students. There were a lot of girls to check out. Also, my sister had girlfriends only two years younger than me. Time and quantity were on my side

Sara was in the 7th grade at Danbury Junior High School. She became friends with many new girls and spoke to them for hours on the telephone. Sometimes, they were guests in our home. I was nervous about being introduced to one of

Sara's friends even though we had talked on the phone a couple of times. Her name was Lynne Paris. She sounded cute when we spoke. How someone could "sound" cute is beyond my realm of understanding now, but it made perfect sense to me then.

I met Lynne at Sara's and Gilberte's (our next door neighbor) 13th birthday party in April 1965. Sara and Gilberte shared the same day and year of birth. To celebrate the occasion of their first teen year, they held a party at the American Legion hall on Elm Street in downtown Danbury. I volunteered to be the deejay for the party. I combined all of our 45 rpm records into a stack and played tunes on an old phonograph all afternoon long. Among the favorites of the day were "The Last Time" by the Rolling Stones, "Help Me Rhonda" by the Beach Boys, and The Beatles' "Eight Days A Week". Sometime between spinning the disks of British invasion and Surf music, I was introduced to Lynne. Instantly, she reminded me of a typical English girl, like Patti Boyd, with high cheek bones, long straight hair, and bangs across her forehead. She *was* cute.

That night, I sat down, and composed a long note to Lynne. The words flowed effortlessly from my pen. Time has erased the essence of this letter from memory, but I felt free to write anything I wanted, humorous or otherwise. The missive to Lynne marked the beginning of a habit. From that point on, it became easier for me to write down my thoughts and feelings instead of proclaiming them verbally. Also, I began writing down the days, hours, and minutes elapsed since last seeing my female correspondents, as well as annotating the time of day I started and finished the note. All were written neatly in the upper right hand corner of the page. It was fun to write, but the note must have been a deal breaker for Lynne. We never became a romantic couple, but much more important in the long run, we've remained friends for over 50 years.

As the summer of 1965 approached, all eyes turned towards the beach. Danbury was the site of one of the country's largest man-made lakes, Candlewood. The town had a park on the lake open to all Danbury residents. Every year each Danbury student received a button that served as a free pass to the Lake. The park contained a long stretch of sandy beach, a large lawn with picnic tables, snack bar, and a lifeguard hut that also had a loudspeaker on top of its roof. Rock and Roll from Top 40 AM radio played all day. Most weekdays, Sara and I would walk to the bus stop a mile away on the corner of Coalpit Hill and South Street, located in front of Nejame's Food Market, just across the street from Buddy's Mobil gas station. The bus took us on the four mile trip to the lake.

Danbury Town Park on Candlewood Lake was THE place to be for a Danbury teen. It was a perfect location for young people to swim, listen to music, goof around, smoke cigarettes, and eat inordinate amounts of hamburgers, hot dogs, and snow cones. One could find several friends and acquaintances on any given day at the Town Park.

I was in my element there...spending a lot of time in the water, swimming out to one of the floats, slithering down the slide, and jumping into the water. Some days, my mother picked us up after she got out of work. Other times, we took the bus back to Coalpit Hill and South Street. On the return trip by bus, we got out in front of Carvel's Ice Cream store.

Sara and I walked the rest of the way home with an ice cream cone in hand. The snack was always gone before we arrived at Putnam Drive, thus saving us from listening to Mom's "you'll spoil your appetite" lecture.

I met a lot of girls at the lake, but still had trouble connecting with any of them on a more-than-friends basis. One day I met a girl named Darcy, who I hung out with all day at the beach. I thought she was really cool. Sara and I mentioned her name to one another at the supper table that night. That's when my father looked me in the eye and said that Darcy was my third cousin. A small lecture about cousins and in-breeding began. Geez Dad, she was just a girl I met at the lake, I'm not marrying her. Parents could be such a drag.

The greatest Rock and Roll single of all time emerged in June 1965. It's not the best song ever written and didn't remain at #1 as long as others have, but nothing can compare to the wild pulsating teenage angst of "Satisfaction" by the Rolling Stones. No other 3 minute song from the middle 1960s captures youthful frustration, sexual and otherwise, so well. The searing guitar of Keith Richard, tribal beat of Charlie Watts, and manic sound of Mick Jagger gave voice to disappointment, confusion and unrequited love. A wave of excitement ripples through me whenever I hear it today.

There was controversy about the lyrics of the song's final verse. It's absurd to think about it now, but radio stations censored the last verse of "Satisfaction" because the singer was "trying to make some girl." In the early 1980s, no one blinked an eye when Olivia Newton John wanted to get "physical", but in 1965 Mick Jagger was perceived as a threat to the youth of the nation.

"Satisfaction" elevated the Rolling Stones to new heights in popularity, particularly among boys. It was somewhat difficult to be a male Beatles fan during the early years. Many guys liked the Fab Four and their music, but were reluctant to admit it. After all, The Beatles were a group of guys that girls fainted and cried over. That was not a very macho image for boy fans concerned about peer pressure. Beginning with "Satisfaction" the Rolling Stones became my second favorite band and continued to be for many years to come. However, as the story goes in the lyrics, I couldn't get any satisfaction either...that is until later that year.

A month or so after school started, Sara told me about a girl in her class that she thought I might like. Her name was "Cindy". I was intrigued, but this was a girl that my sister was recommending, not someone I liked first on my own. That gave me pause for thought. But what the heck...I said OK and began a note correspondence with Cindy via delivery by Sara. Writing notes in school has disappeared in the age of emails, texts, and Facebook, but "the note", which was written on lined notebook paper and folded so the corners tucked into one another, was the mode of communication among students in 1965.

It wasn't until much later that I discovered Sara's motivation in matching me up with Cindy wasn't entirely altruistic. She considered Cindy a rival for a boy she liked. By introducing Cindy to me, she hoped to eliminate the competition. And it worked. Our notes led to meeting Cindy at a dance sponsored by the St. James Episcopal Church on West Street in Danbury. I couldn't dance to save my life (still can't), but somehow Cindy and I hit it off on the dance floor.

We met, exchanged pleasantries, and shouted in each other's ears to be heard above the live band playing in the dance hall. Although Cindy was almost two years younger than me, she looked older. She had reddish brown hair and was a bit boisterous and bossy, but there was definitely an attraction between the two of us. Before I knew what hit me, a romance developed. We kept in touch with notes and many long afternoon phone calls. Yet, we still hadn't been on an "official" date.

During 1965, I became a big fan of James Bond movies. I saw "Goldfinger" three times in the same week and watched a twin-bill of "Dr. No" and "From Russia With Love". 007 was my idea of the suave assured man who always got the girl he wanted. If I were like Bond, even in a small way, I would always have luck with girls. Bond's daring and sophistication produced numerous imitation movies, e.g. the Matt Helm series with Dean Martin and Flint films with James Coburn. I took Cindy to one of those poor man's James Bond flicks for our first date.

I remember very little about the movie. Instead, I was concentrating on Cindy and the way her hair brushed against me every time she moved. We talked incessantly, much to the annoyance of people sitting around us, but we didn't care. Then a thought entered my mind...hey, put your arm around her. This idea was immediately countered by cold feet. Eventually, in delicate stages of maneuvering, I put my arm around her as she rested her head on my shoulder. This was much easier than I anticipated. We remained that way for awhile each waiting for the other to make or break. And then the moment arrived. Not a word was said. Our lips met briefly, but long enough for us to know what was happening.

Every fiber of my being was on fire. A jolt of electricity flashed inside me from my head to my toes. We kissed again...this time longer than the first. WOW, this was great, even better than I imagined. I was on top of the world. This was it...no more being insecure about girls...now I even knew how to kiss.

I asked Cindy to "go steady" a few days after our first kiss. She said yes without hesitation. Our sweet teen romance was in bloom. Things were happening at a rapid pace in my personal life and in the world.

It was good to be young and alive in 1965.

CHAPTER TEN---A Hot Day's Night

One spring day, my sister ran into my room with a copy of "16 Magazine" clutched in her hands. Excitedly, Sara pushed a page in front of my face. It was a list of cities for the upcoming Beatles' American Tour. The first concert was set for Sunday, August 15, 1965 at Shea Stadium in Flushing, New York. We were ecstatic at the prospect of seeing the Fabs in person.

Sara and I missed The Beatles at Forest Hills Tennis Stadium during the summer of 1964. Our Aunt Ruth, who lived in Manhattan, tried to get us tickets, but the concert was already sold out. In 1965 we were determined to get the tickets ourselves and see the Beatles in August. But how? I was almost 15 years old and Sara was 13. We had no idea what to do. After many inquiries we found a place called the M & M Ticket Agency on Liberty St. in Danbury. Not only did they have tickets for the concert, but there was a package deal that included a round trip bus ride to Shea Stadium.

The ticket agency bought up several rows of seats in the Upper Deck. The price of a ticket was $5.65. That was a hefty amount in 1965. Many of our friends' parents thought it was too expensive and wouldn't allow their kids to go. My parents didn't have a lot of money, but Sara and I made such a strong case for our going to Shea that they agreed we could attend. Also, our good friend and next-door neighbor, Gilberte Najamy, had permission to go. The three of us went to the agency, bought our tickets, and paid a few dollars more for the bus ride.

However, this happy arrangement had one downside. My mother was apprehensive about letting her two children venture into the bustling metropolis of Flushing alone. Therefore, my parents volunteered to be chaperones on one of the chartered busses going to Shea Stadium. And guess which bus they rode? Yep...that's right. Time has not erased from my mind the image of Dad clapping along to a rousing vocal rendition of "Eight Days A Week" from a bunch of girls on the bus (and this was music he supposedly hated).

Actually, having my parents on board the bus wasn't as bad as I thought it would be. They left us alone and seemed to have a good time. However, Martha and Campbell didn't have tickets to the concert. While we were inside attending the show they walked over to the New York World's Fair. Shea Stadium, the newly constructed home of my favorite baseball team, the New York Mets, had been part of the initial construction for the Fair and was right next door.

August 15th arrived. During the previous school year, I washed the greasy kid-stuff out of my hair for good and began combing it down. That Sunday morning, I washed my hair twice to make sure it would gently cascade across my forehead and fall just short of my eyes. My clothes had to be just right. I wore a maroon Henley shirt which was collarless with a white border around the neck and under the top buttons. I thought I looked cool on a very hot night. In fact, the entire Summer of 1965 was hot with a major drought in the New York metropolitan area. Conservation of water was urged on TV commercials and newspaper ads. Throughout the night of August 15th a blimp circled Shea Stadium with an electronic sign flashing the message, "Save Water."

When we arrived at the ball park there were thousands of kids from Connecticut, New York, and New Jersey. I had never been in one place with so many people my age. The sheer numbers of kids in my generation hit me for the first time. Most of the concert goers were girls. For me, only a week away from my 15th birthday, this was like Heaven. Girls everywhere I looked. Many wore flower print short-hemmed dresses and skirts. Most of them had long straight hair with bangs across their foreheads...the classic mid-Sixties look for girls.

Sara, Gilberte, and I found our seats in Section 12, Row C of the Upper Deck between home plate and third base. Seated in front of us were Wendy, Carolyn, Sue, and Sheila... girls I knew from high school. We talked for as long as we could. However, as the stadium filled up it became increasingly difficult to hold a conversation. Thunderous, ground shaking jets taking off from nearby LaGuardia airport flew right over the ball park. Girls started screaming when anyone walked across the ball field, drowning out the sound of the jets. Some started crying. Expectations and emotions were running high.

I have no doubt that the opening acts of Brenda Holloway, the King Curtis Band, Cannibal and the Headhunters, and Sounds Inc. all had their musical merits, but the crowd was bored by them and couldn't wait for that part of the show to be over. My only clear memory is that of Cannibal and the Headhunters singing "Land of 1,000 Dances", which had been a big NYC area hit earlier in the year. Otherwise, the audience had no use for those bands.

At last the big moment arrived. Ed Sullivan introduced The Beatles to the massive crowd and the noise level rose to new heights. It was the most intense moment of sound in my life. The cacophony of screaming, crying and wailing assaulted my ears and sent waves of vibrations all over my body. The continuous flashing of camera bulbs throughout Shea Stadium provided a massive light show for my eyes, but my gaze was fixed on the field. Emerging from the Mets' dugout were four tiny figures. Quickly, they ascended the stage. Three of them strapped on their guitars and the last person sat behind the drum kit. A year and a half after their first visit to the United States, I was watching The Beatles live...in person.

The noise was so overwhelming that I didn't know The Beatles had started to play or what song they were singing. Someone yelled it was "Twist and Shout", but by then they were into their second song of the night, "She's A Woman." I had a slight auditory advantage over the girls. I wasn't screaming. Therefore, my voice wasn't adding to the sounds bombarding my head. This enabled me to hear the song introductions better than those who sat next to me. I heard Paul introduce the next song, "I Feel Fine", and recognized its familiar opening riff.

The Beatles went on to perform, "Dizzy Miss Lizzy", "Ticket To Ride", "Everybody's Trying To Be My Baby", and "Can't Buy Me Love." Paul asked the crowd to join in and clap during the latter song. I heard bits and pieces of them all...from the strong and steady rhythm guitar of "Dizzy Miss Lizzy" to the vocal fade-out of "Ticket To Ride."

The Beatles looked quite small from our upper deck "nose-bleed" seats. I couldn't see their facial expressions with the naked eye. At different intervals, Sara and I shared a pair of powerful binoculars. I could see more detail whenever I looked through the field glasses. The Beatles were wearing brown jackets with black pants. They were sweating profusely just like the rest of us. At one point, one of the girls seated in front of me said that Mick Jagger was in the dugout watching the show. The popularity of the Rolling Stones was soaring due to their big summertime hit song, "Satisfaction." I pointed the lens of my binoculars towards the dugout area and saw a young guy with long hair, but it was impossible to say who he was. Sara insisted it was Mick and that he waved to her. Decades later we found out that Mick Jagger and Keith Richard were there.

Just before the introduction to "Baby's In Black", fans climbed over the outfield wall from the parking lot and scurried toward the stage. They never had a chance. The police ran after them as John Lennon remarked, "Looky there", into his open mike. John, Paul, and George "waltzed" with their guitars during the middle eight. However, the next song was a complete mystery. No one sitting around us knew what it was. Ringo was singing, but we didn't recognize the tune. It was "Act Naturally" which had not aired on US radio (it was on the UK "Help" album) and wouldn't be released until the following month as the "B" side of the "Yesterday" single.

Then something strange happened. The constant noise of the night wasn't as loud. Girls were becoming exhausted... their voices giving out from the strain. The sound quality of the music was still far from perfect, but the last three songs of the evening were easier to hear. One of my favorite songs, "A Hard Day's Night" came next. I watched The Beatles sing and play through the binoculars for most of the song. Prior to seeing this concert, I could only view what a film producer or TV camera decided to show the audience.

It was a heady experience to control my observation of the band on stage.

Then I experienced some pain. The Beatles launched into "Help", their current single. Sara loved that song. We kept passing the binoculars back and forth. Right before the third verse (a repeat of the first) when the tempo slows down a bit for John to sing, "When I was younger, so much younger than today", Sara yelled into my ear, "I have to watch John sing this." She grabbed the binoculars from my hands. Unfortunately, the strap was still around my neck. I spent the remainder of "Help" choking. Sara was so into the moment that she wasn't aware of my predicament. Visions of newspaper headlines reading, "BOY STRANGLED BY SISTER AT BEATLES CONCERT", ran through my head. Finally, "Help" was over and I was able to breathe again.

My favorite moment of the entire concert was the show's finale, "I'm Down." Knowing that it was the last song of the evening, I commandeered the field glasses for most of it. The performance of that tune was unique for The Beatles because John played the electric organ instead of a guitar. I watched him run his elbow across the keyboard and said to myself, "What is he doing?" Throughout most of the song, John joked with George, who shared a mike with him for back-up vocals. Both were laughing hard as John continued to play the organ with his elbow and wave to the crowd. Years later, this same sequence was shown in vivid detail on the Beatles Anthology while Ringo explained that John "got a little crazy" that night. It was obvious...The Beatles were overwhelmed by the Shea Stadium experience as well.

And then it was over. The concert was only about 40 minutes in length, but it seemed much longer. It is now common knowledge that The Beatles began to tire of performing during the 1965 tour. In some cities they put on less than a stellar show, realizing they could not be heard well. The band going through the motions occurred as the tour progressed, but on August 15, 1965 at Shea Stadium, The Beatles had a lot of fun playing in front of 56,000 people.

We, their ardent fans, had the time of our lives watching them.

CHAPTER ELEVEN---Lights Out

When we weren't watching our favorite TV program, "The Soupy Sales Show", on late weekday afternoons, Sara and I did chores while listening to Dad's old radio and the hits of the day. By the fall of 1965, there were two radio stations in New York City vying for airwave supremacy...the All-Americans of WABC and the WMCA Good Guys. My first allegiance was to WABC and its afternoon disk jockey, Dan Ingram. Dan was called "the thinking man's deejay." He made humorous remarks about songs and commercials and often told jokes containing thinly veiled double-entendre. And, amazing for 1965, he got away with it.

Dan Ingram always introduced the new weekly WABC Top Ten list of songs on Tuesday afternoons. There were several times during my high school years when I stayed home "sick" on a Tuesday to be among the first to know which song was Number One. Most listeners found out what songs were in the Top Ten by tuning in Cousin Brucie on Tuesday nights, but I just HAD to know before everyone else.

Late Tuesday afternoons involved a different kind of musical interlude for Sara. She received lessons on an upright piano in our living room. Her teacher, Miss Casazza, traveled each Tuesday to Putnam Drive from her home on Clapboard Ridge Road. Now, I regret not taking piano lessons, but in the early 60s I thought the piano was a sissy thing and wanted no part of it. Also, I resented that Sara's lessons interfered with my household activities. I had to be very quiet while Sara plunked away on the ivories. One time, I had to go to a neighbor's house to watch the All-Star baseball game when they were still held in the afternoon. Doesn't sound like a big deal now, but I was angry about it then.

It was a typical Tuesday in early November 1965. Sara's piano lesson ended around 5:00 PM. We were both excited because Mom and Dad promised to pick up a pizza on their way home from work. On the south side of Danbury there were two places to get pizza...Napoli's on Main St near the New York Bakery and Angelo's on South St. near Nejame's IGA food market. That night, our pizza was coming from Napoli's.

Sara and I flew into action as soon as Miss Casazza left. Mom and Dad would soon be home and we had to set the table and get the drinks ready. We turned on the old radio which was located on a desk in the dining room. Every afternoon, Dan Ingram played older instrumentals to end his program or as a lead-in to the news. That day it was "Up The Lazy River." Suddenly the song began to fade out, then surge louder, only to fade away again. Initially, we thought the ancient radio was on its last legs and about to die, but then Ingram told his audience, "...something strange is going on with our transmitter folks..." Night settled quickly outside as the living room lights dimmed. The radio fell silent as the lamps went out completely.

We looked outside. The absence of street lights near the darkened homes made Putnam Drive look like a ghost town. Our parents arrived home a couple of minutes later. They told us about driving down Main Street while traffic lights, street lamps and neon signs went black one by one. Soon, the families on Putnam Drive began to gather outside. No one knew what was going on. It felt like we were part of the Twilight Zone episode in which the people on Maple Street lose electricity and eventually their sanity. Finally, a neighbor with a transistor radio located a broadcasting station. We learned that this was not an isolated local event. It was the largest power blackout ever to occur in the United States. The November 9th power outage affected most of the Northeast and its major metropolitan cities. New York City was plunged into darkness at the height of rush hour.

The full extent of the electrical breakdown left us in awe. Fierce lightning, ice storms, and heavy winds were the usual causes of power failures, but this time was different. It was a quiet and peaceful November evening...no rain, snow or wind. A primordial eeriness enveloped the night. What was happening here? Had some natural catastrophe triggered this widespread blackout? Was it deliberate? Did our government shut off the power because an enemy air attack was imminent?

Calmness prevailed once we understood that the entire Northeast power-grid had been forced off due to the malfunction of an electrical sub-station near Buffalo New York. Still, there was an air of mystery about being outdoors without lights, listening to people gab, gossip and wonder. It reminded me of when I was younger and joined other kids on crisp October nights, flashlights in hand, to play Halloween inspired pranks on unsuspecting neighbors. This time there was no ringing of doorbells or soaping car windows. On my street, as well as in other neighborhoods across the Northeast, people were chatting with the folks next door, across the street, or in the next apartment. Fathers and mothers, home from a hard day's work, were sitting down and talking with their kids. Without electricity to power the stove or turn on the TV, families were enjoying each other's company. The Catone family ate pizza by candlelight that night.

On November 9, 1965, one of the busiest regions on Earth was brought to a standstill. Many Americans relaxed and questioned the hustle and bustle of their everyday lives. However, that retrospection didn't last long. Once the lights returned, our country never slowed down again. Whatever technology could do was accepted as a blessing. People pledged their loyalty to anything that seemed to make life easier and faster. It didn't matter how a goal was accomplished as long as got done quickly. Worshipping the golden calf of technology became a ritual regardless of its overall effect on society.

My first experience with the increased rapidity of American life occurred less than a year after the Northeast Blackout. McDonald's restaurants were becoming more numerous nationwide, but there were none in Danbury. One day I noticed a McDonald's as we drove on Route 7 in Norwalk. Mom was driving and I asked her to stop there for lunch. She waited in the car as I walked through the golden arches for the first time. I ordered a hamburger, French fries and a drink. Less than a minute later my food was ready. When the cashier told me it was mine, I did a double-take. My brain was unable to comprehend that the hamburger and fries could be ready so fast. How could this be? I felt sure that she made a mistake. The meal had to belong to someone else...not enough cooking time had elapsed for it to be my order. When she insisted that the hamburger was mine, I took the bag in disbelief and walked outside to the family car. I half-expected to find the Candid Camera crew awaiting my arrival.

My mother said, "You're back already?"

However, as your average impatient teenager, I was quite impressed by things happening faster. Daily, there were new experiences coming my way. I had a girl friend, saw The Beatles at Shea Stadium, and got a hamburger into my mouth within minutes of ordering it. Making out, Rock and Roll and fast food...a boy's dream come true.

But then, something began to tug at my brain. My conscience demanded equal time.

CHAPTER TWELVE---Teach Your Children

My parents were Republicans, but I never held it against them. Mom voted for the GOP because my father voted that way. Martha had her opinions, but to keep peace in the family she sided with Camp when it came to elections. Both Mom and Dad voted for Eisenhower in 1952 and 1956 and Nixon in 1960. My father didn't like FDR or Truman. When I asked Dad what the "S" in Harry S. Truman stood for, he replied, "Stinkpot." I believed him for about 4 seconds.

I knew nothing about politics when I was a freshman in 1964. I wanted Barry Goldwater to beat Lyndon Johnson. My parents were voting for him, I thought, therefore he must be good. That's how deep my reasons went for supporting Goldwater. How dorky I must have appeared to my classmates as I walked around the halls of the brand new Danbury High School with an "AuH_2O" bumper sticker emblazoned on my Social Studies notebook.

In 1965, I was the All-American boy. I knew that my country was the best one in the entire world. I knew that other nations envied our democracy and technical prowess. I knew that the United States faced dire threats from communism. I had no doubt that my country always told the truth and was never wrong. I believed it whole-heartedly. The possibility that the United States might be wrong in the pursuit of its policies never occurred to me. However, by mid-1965 something began to change inside my head. It was subliminal at first, a brief scene on the back-burner of my mind. Then it grew quickly until it occupied an entire lobe of my brain labeled "**Vietnam.**"

In late 1965, I realized that there was something big happening with young people in America. It started when I went to see The Beatles at Shea Stadium in August. There were thousands of teenagers there. I had never seen such a gathering of people my age. It was evident that all the teens I knew in Danbury had counterparts everywhere, and then some. Most people associate themselves with their ethnicity or religion, but I never felt comfortable in identifying with either the Jewish or Italian part of my heritage. Instead, I took bits and pieces from each as part of my background. However, I felt a stronger alliance and bond with the emerging Sixties Generation. That was us. That was me.

Things were changing fast in the USA. American Rock and Roll bands, such as the Byrds and Beau Brummels, were wearing their hair long. So were their fans. The Byrds and the Turtles recorded songs written by a singer/composer named Bob Dylan. I didn't know much about Dylan except that he wrote "Blowin' In The Wind" (we sang it in Junior High music class) and had a six minute hit single called "Like A Rolling Stone." Simultaneously, shows about young people and their lifestyles began to appear on TV. There was one about a group of kids who wore their hair long and had alternative views on work, play, and society in general. Although no one referred to them yet as "hippies", that's what they were, living in a building together as a community in New York City. They shared responsibilities and worked together for the group. They were a family and yet there was no head of household. ..no leader...just unity.

Another TV program concentrated on a Folk/Rock band, the Magicians, during a typical day in their lives. The members of the group were funny, sometimes serious, and I related to their ups and downs. The Magicians never made it "big" in the music world, but two members, Gary Bonner and Alan Gordon, composed several of the Turtles' late Sixties songs, including "Happy Together" and "She'd Rather Be With Me". Although most media reports of young people were limited and often didn't go beyond clichéd descriptions, it was the beginning of TV's coverage of a generation coming into its own.

The Folk/Rock music of protest became popular. There was one song in particular that had an impact upon me in the early fall of 1965. It got me thinking about injustices and double-standards in our society. It was called, "Eve Of Destruction", written by P.F. Sloan and sung by Barry McGuire. To say it was sung isn't entirely correct. When McGuire appeared on NBC's weekly pop music show, "Hullabaloo", he spit out each word of the song in a gruff raspy voice. The lyrics growled of things gone wrong in the world, the hypocrisies of war, and the futile hatred which existed among nationalities and religions. Today, "Eve of Destruction" is considered to be an over-simplistic song with a laundry list of complaints and no plan of action. To my mind, the meaning of the song was obvious. People should take to the streets and demand that government change its ways. Young people had to sound the alarm. And I wanted to be part of that response.

TV showed college students questioning whether the United States military should be fighting in Vietnam. The idea of war confused me from an early age. I couldn't understand why people fought...why anyone would want to join the army. It made no sense to me. However, the idea that America could be wrong in a military situation was a new one. I began to pay attention to campus antiwar protests by students only a few years older than me. They received harsh reactions from politicians and many older Americans. I had empathy for their cause, although I wasn't well-versed in all the facts.

I didn't know about the modern history of Vietnam and why the United States was involved in warfare with that nation. My high school classmates didn't have any answers even though some of their brothers and cousins were in the army over there. We were told that the troops were fighting to preserve our freedom, but we didn't know anything about what was happening in Southeast Asia and why the United States should be there.

So, I did some research on my own at the library. I learned that Vietnam was once a unified nation, but had been the victim of invasion, colonization, and occupation by China, France and Japan respectively. Their resistance movement against the Japanese during World War II was led by Ho Chi Minh, who in 1965 was still the leader in the northern part of the country. After the war was over, France tried to reassert its colonial authority which led to fighting with the Viet Minh, forerunners to the communist Viet Cong guerillas. Eventually, France was defeated in 1954. Shortly thereafter, the United States became involved by propping up a new a government in the southern part of Vietnam and coming to its aid in the form of intelligence officers and Special Forces to fight the communists.

I discovered that elections were supposed to be held in Vietnam no later than July 1956, per the Geneva Conference of 1954 (when Vietnam defeated the French at Dien Bien Phu). However, the Vietnamese leader backed by the United States refused to hold elections because he knew that Ho Chi Minh would win. The United States stood by that decision and no elections were held. That stunned me. My country, the United States, the world's greatest democracy, actively participated in stopping a democratic election that would determine the government of Vietnam. I had a difficult time understanding that the USA, the same country that rescued Europe during World War I and the entire world in World War II, would forsake democracy because their candidate might not win. That tactic went against every lesson I had learned in U.S. history.

In 1965, I didn't understand what the peace movement was up against. It all came down to Dwight Eisenhower's warning. In his farewell speech as president in January 1961, Ike told the American people to beware of the increasing power of the "military-industrial complex." His prophesy came true when both the US military and major corporations ran amok in Vietnam. We became entrenched in Vietnam with no end in sight, and no stop to the killing on both sides. War was good for business. Unfortunately, the Military-Industrial complex continues to control many aspects of our lives now in the 21st century.

My new understanding of Vietnam begged the question...why was the United States sending its young men to kill and be killed in a country involved in a civil war? It became evident to me that the USA had no business being there. However, I was hesitant to declare that awareness publicly. I got the message from many of my teachers, some classmates, and the media that it was unpatriotic to question why the United States was in Vietnam. Also, it was clear to me that one should be cautious in making waves over this issue, especially when I saw film footage of demonstrators clubbed and dragged away by police.

Protesters on college campuses were held in contempt by many. They were called traitors and much worse. As a 15 yr. old boy, who wanted to fit in with his classmates, I felt conflicted over my increasingly negative view of the USA in Vietnam. Peer pressure is powerful. However, no single act of defiance impressed me more than draft card burning by antiwar protesters. It was a brave statement. They put their futures on the line by risking imprisonment to show their discontent with the war in Vietnam. This particular act of civil disobedience reminded me of the American colonists throwing tea in Boston harbor. In fact, it struck me as being a primal American impulse to show one's disgust by doing something so graphic. All across the United States, my generation was questioning why we were invading another nation. We were doing what other generations had failed to do...taking authority to task for sending young men off to war. Maybe, we would be the ones to stop this craziness once and for all.

It was a teacher who helped me to articulate my thoughts.

Edith Thor was my English teacher during my second year of high school. She was the most unconventional teacher I encountered during my high school years. In 1965, Mrs. Thor was in her late forties or early fifties. Often, she wore wool skirts with turtleneck tops and sweaters, often accented by a necklace featuring an African or Caribbean motif. Mrs. Thor's hair had a tendency to get a bit rumpled and fall into her eyes, reminiscent of the photos I'd seen of Amelia

Earhardt's tousled look on a windy airport runway. Her laid-back demeanor and mode of dress was quite Bohemian...early hippie.

Mrs. Thor allowed us to be individuals, explore our own ideas, and be ourselves as much as possible within a traditional classroom setting. She earned my respect at the beginning of the school year when she acknowledged my desire to be called "Marc" instead of my given name, "Marcus." None of my other teachers would let me do that.

She trusted her students' inclinations. I recall a very artistic classmate named John, who Mrs. Thor encouraged to include original drawings in his homework. She even allowed him to read the lyrics of the Byrd's then current song, "Turn Turn Turn", to the rest of the class. Granted, the words were taken from the Bible, but in 1965 it was very unusual for a teacher to let a pupil read the words from any Rock song to his classmates.

I never got to know Mrs. Thor very well. Our paths seldom crossed when I wasn't in her English class. Most of my studies took place on the second floor of "D" Building and her classroom was two floors above. I don't recall speaking to her again after the 1965-1966 school year, but she had an everlasting impact upon me nonetheless.

One day in early December 1965, Mrs. Thor gave the class an assignment to write a short story. The due date was the day we came back from Christmas break. A few audible moans and groans were heard among my classmates, including yours truly, as one student raised his hand to ask if the short story should have a particular theme.

Mrs. Thor replied, "It can be about anything you want."

No teacher had ever uttered those words to us before. "Anything you want." There was a magical lilt to the phrase...but also an edge to it. Edith Thor gave her students carte blanche on the assignment, but with freedom came the responsibility to craft a tale worthy of the honor. After a few days, certain images...visions...began to roll through my head. There were scenes of recent college student protests, draft card burnings, and young people confronting authority figures. At last, my anger about the Vietnam War had a place to go. Mrs. Thor's short story request gave me the perfect opportunity to express my views on paper. I could incorporate my discontent about the Vietnam War within a fictional framework, yet in reality it was an opinion piece. A great idea...but did I have enough confidence to pull it off? Slowly, the story line evolved...the issue of dissent became the focus of a young man arrested for burning his draft card.

Reproduced below, containing some spelling and punctuation changes, but with the original untouched and unvarnished sentences, is the short story, *"Who Is Right?"*, which was written when I was age 15 in December 1965:

As the crowd diminished, and men went back to their places of business, and women and children returned home, the paddy wagon left the scene, racing for the nearest police station. The wagon swished through the wet streets, and did not seem to disturb the outside world, but then, all the world wasn't outside of this vehicle; a small minority was inside. Bums, the supposedly adult world called them. Extremists, some of their own generation called them. Disturbed young men, the psycho-analysts called them.

One of them, Alfie Lansing, could not possibly be called a bum because he came from a wealthy family. Sure, he had long hair, and if anyone remarked about it, he'd explain that his father's and grandfather's generations were the only two generations of history to have short hair. Thus, the long hair was merely a revival of past history. Now, can you call a person like him a bum, or can you? A small part of his own generation did not coincide with his thoughts, so the term "Extremist" was centered upon him. The psycho-analysts referred to him as disturbed because they just didn't have any other answers. What are Alfie's, and the others' problem? Let Alfie tell it to you, and the world, as he is interviewed by a psychiatrist down at the Police Station where he has just been charged with inciting a riot.

"What happened to you today, young man?", asked a man about a score older than the boy he questioned.

"Sir, my friends and I are lovers of peace, who wish to stop all wars!"

"How do you, and your friends, intend to do this?"

"We try to tell the world our views, but no one listens! They never do even though what we say concerns their welfare and stability."

"How do you account for that, Mr. Lansing?" asked the big bad adult to the small lamb boy.

"Well, we tell them that the war in Asia should stop before it spreads into a major war. But they don't listen to us, they, the people who have made the atom bomb, they who have made the hydrog..."

"Now that isn't true son, and you know it! You say that the generation before you made the atom bomb. My poor deluded boy, the "A" bomb was in the making before I was born!"

"Yes, that's true, " Alfie admitted, "But did they come together with other people of different lands to make laws for its use or non-use? No, they did not."

"Son, it's hard to have mixed peoples come together, it has always been."

"That's why I'm here today, right now, because my friends and I were protesting and telling the world to negotiate before it is too late."

"You also burned your draft and classification card," remarked the witty man whose eyes sparkled with delight, thinking he had it all over this boy.

"Sir, I did because without that you cannot draw attention, and without attention no one listens or cares."

"Are you and your friends lovers of peace, or afraid to fight if you have to?" asked the frustrated psychiatrist.

"I have a couple of answers for you, sir. One is that we don't want to fight in a war which is not wholeheartedly supported by all the people of this land. The second is we wish to live full and long lives, and we want our children to live full lives also! A war can mean the end in our young lives. Do you want to die like that sir, or are you happy that your generation caused this situation?", asked the slowly-burning-inside Alfie.

"Young man, as I told you before, it wasn't entirely our fault. You realize, of course, that what you did is a federal offense, and you can be sentenced to a prison."

"I am not afraid to be punished, sir!"

"Do you mind if we change the subject to your own personal life?"

"I have a feeling that you are afraid to hear my opinions sir."

Overlooking Alfie's last remark, he said, "How old are you son, and what are your aims in life?"

"You are fighting me sir, aren't you?"

"Son, I just want to see what makes you tick."

"You're afraid that you might hear something that you might not want to hear. The adult is afraid of the adolescent. The adult has always been; sir, I'm eighteen years old. My goal is to help the world towards peace, but I can't do it alone. I need you and everybody in this country to help me. If you ask me, you're the one who is afraid, afraid to help . You sit on your haunches and let everybody do everything for you. The adult doesn't have it easy, but a lot easier than we do. Just remember, when your generation is old and gray, and when you extend your hand for help, who will be there? No one, because we will remember how we were treated, and you will die a slow, maddening death after you live your slow meaningless life."

"I won't take this from someone like you, a bum like you, who is still wet behind the ears. I just won't stand for it! Guard, lock this poor boy up."

As the guard took him away, Alfie said, "You can't win!"

That's it exactly! The adult, supposedly mature, and the most intelligent type of human being, is always right in his own eyes. He can do no wrong. When encircled by a threat to crush his security, he makes excuses and insults. Now, I'm not saying Alfie is right or wrong, but from this essay, you are to judge for yourself.

And so it seems as Alfie's hearing came up that he actually burned a copy of his draft card. He was freed, but not for long. He was drafted, and in less than three months he was over in Vietnam fighting, possibly dying, for the adults who had so much respect for him.

Now we end the story, but is this really the end? For Alfie is now a soldier fighting because he has to. He is doing his duty according to adult American standards, but why did they treat him so unkindly?

Kind of hypocritical! Isn't it?

During the early stages of protest against the Vietnam War, the general public doubted the veracity and honesty of those who questioned our government's policies. I reflected this view by pitting Alfie against an adult authority figure who questioned the young man's motivations. Today, I am surprised by my very harsh treatment of adults in *"Who Is Right?"* and seeing how pissed off I was at the time. Thinking back on it, I wasn't angry with the adults I knew, but rather with those who controlled the government and military. I recall being particularly incensed by an editorial cartoon that showed two protesters with long hair and no facial features. The caption insulted their appearance, but ignored the reasons why they were protesting. The first person says to the other, "Are you gonna burn your draft card?" The second person replies, "No, I'm a girl."

As *"Who Is Right?"*progressed, Alfie engaged the nameless psychiatrist in conversation about generational blame for the world's overall condition. Youth put the elder on the defensive. But, the story had a sad ending. Alfie Lansing was drafted into the Army and sent to Vietnam. His fate went undisclosed, but the people who pulled his strings were exposed for their lack of caring about him except as fodder in the war effort.

I was proud and excited about my English writing assignment, but became apprehensive when the time arrived to hand in my story to Mrs. Thor. She was a cool person for a middle-aged teacher, but I wasn't sure about her reactions to my writings. I feared that she might disagree with the politics of *"Who Is Right?"* and that would affect her grading. A week later, Mrs. Thor handed back my short story with a big red "A" written across the top of the first page. I was beaming.

That day, Mrs. Thor took me aside for a few minutes to discuss my short story. She declared that it was wrong to send US troops to Vietnam, thus becoming the first adult of my acquaintance to take such a position. Mrs.Thor spoke about the horror of all wars and that each person needed to do their part in the world's quest for peace. She praised me for the depth of perception in *"Who Is Right?"* and said it was always important for a writer to stick to his convictions,

"Always write what you believe in", she said.

By expressing her opinions so candidly, Mrs. Thor inspired me to write about those matters close to my heart. Even today, I can't write about something that doesn't interest me or arouse my passions. Whenever I try to write about a subject or theme that means very little to me, it comes out bland, unappealing and phony. I don't know if my writings about political and social themes would have continued if Mrs. Thor hadn't given me that nudge when I needed it.

That's why I remember her fondly over 50 years later.

CHAPTER THIRTEEN---Just A State Of Mind

A female classmate told me that I resembled Zal Yanovsky from the Lovin' Spoonful. Well, that was all I needed to hear...a girl thought I looked like a Rock Star. That was so boss! The Spoonful wore colorful clothing with lots of polka dot shirts. Soon, I owned a maroon shirt with large white polka dots and a blue silk shirt with "painted" white dots. To top it off, I had a pair of rose-colored "granny" half-frame glasses (just like Spoonful lead singer, John Sebastian).

For a few weeks, I drove my mother crazy asking for a "bleeding" madras windbreaker. Martha gave in. I bought the windbreaker at Feinson's clothing store in Danbury and wore it all over the place. During the winter, I was heavily into corduroy pants...tan, brown and blue...including one that was wide-wale. My colors of choice for shirts were blue and maroon, often I wore a black "dickie" underneath. However, the pride of my wardrobe was a burgundy-colored CPO jacket...buttoned-down denim with long tails that one could wear as a shirt or jacket. Occasionally, I wore the CPO jacket with a pair of baby-blue crushed denim pants and green-brown desert boots. I grew my hair long enough to comb down beyond my eyebrows and into my eyes.

Music remained my main interest in 1966. I bought a cheap folk guitar and tried to teach myself how to play. I learned to pick a little bit and strum some chords from a guitar instruction book, but was never good enough to play in a band. The first thing I learned was the guitar hook from The Beatles "Day Tripper." Eventually, I knew enough major chords to play along with my other records, but that was as far as it went.

By the spring of 1966, the Danbury area was exploding with local Rock bands. The Boss Blues and the Ravens were the most popular, but several of my sophomore classmates were in a couple of high school groups...the Nomads with Kevin Javillonar, Bill Lauf and Joe Koch, and the Mid-Nite Riders with Chris Joy and my home room buddy, Andy "Moose" Bertalovitz. The Nomads were managed by my old Putnam Drive friend, Jerry Lefebvre. Their drummer, Kevin, was one of the first guys in our class to grow his hair long...and he got in trouble because of it.

One day during Mrs. Pierpoint's Geometry class a voice came over the room intercom, "Send Kevin Javillonar to the principal's office." A hushed "uh-oh" fell over my classmates. Whispers among us guessed that Kevin was summoned because of his hair. It's laughable today, but our school officials were upset because Kevin's hair was long enough to fall over his ears and the collar of his shirt. That day he became a hero to us. Kevin was our rebel with a cause.

Garage bands were springing up all over America. My 45 rpm singles playlist in 1966 featured "Psychotic Reaction" by Count Five, "Lies" by the Knickerbockers (many people thought it was The Beatles using a fake name), "96 Tears" by Question Mark and the Mysterians, "Gloria" by Shadows of Knight, "Dirty Water" by the Standells, "Hanky Panky" by Tommy James and the Shondells and "Little Girl" by the Syndicate of Sound.

I played my songs quite loud on an old phonograph in my bedroom. Most of the time, I made sure that my parents weren't home when I played my tunes, but every now and then I was careless. Occasionally, Mom came into my room and told me to turn the music down. I told her it wasn't my fault because the records were already loud before I bought them. That explanation sounded better in theory than in practice. My mother didn't buy it.

My record player could stack three or four 45 rpm records on top of one another and allow each one to drop onto the turntable when the previous record was over. A metal arm kept the records in place while they waited their turn to be played. Leaving the arm in the "up" position, without any records in waiting, returned the stylus to the song on the turntable and let it play over and over again. I did that a lot.

One afternoon, I was playing a new song that had a fantastic guitar hook. It was "Time Won't Let Me" by the Outsiders. I was so entranced by the tune that I left the metal arm up to repeat. I listened to the song for about the fourth or fifth time when suddenly my bedroom door flew open and there stood my mother, her face beet red. I had only seen her that angry on one or two occasions...so I knew she wasn't there to say "hello."

"How can you listen to that same idiotic song so many times in a row?" she screamed.

I didn't even get a chance to feign innocence or ignorance. Without waiting for a reply, Mom walked over to the phonograph, took "Time Won't Let Me" from the turntable, and broke it in half over her knee. Then, as quickly as she came in, she walked out and slammed the door behind her. I patched the record together with some tape, but it never sounded quite the same again.

My sister and I were both teenagers in 1966, a year and a half difference in our ages. Gone were the days of physical fighting and tattle-telling to our parents ("Marc hit me"..."No I didn't"). We liked many of the same things and had in-jokes that our parents didn't understand. Of the two of us, Sara was the extrovert. She was always on the go, happy to be away from home as much as possible. Most week day nights, Sara was on the phone with her friend, Lynne Paris, from the time she got home from school until she went to sleep (taking a short break for supper). Still, she always got her homework done and received good grades. I preferred to be in my room listening to records or the radio...and watching TV. Yes, that's right...a TV...in my room.

I don't remember what persuasive arguments caused my normally austere parents to buy a second television and place it in my room instead of Sara's, but the reasons must have been compelling (or maybe it was because my room was closer to the antenna on the roof). My parents didn't have much money. It had to be expensive to buy that black-and-white TV. I was never one to look a gift horse in the mouth, or to question an uncommon stroke of good luck, therefore I had a TV set in my room. Sara and I shared the TV, but since it was in my room I used it more than she did, often watching programs and movies late into the night, especially on weekends.

In addition to having a TV in my room, I listened to my transistor radio all the time, especially while doing homework and until I went to sleep. AM-Radio signals were much stronger once the sun set. After dark, I listened to WBN-Boston, WKBW-Buffalo, KDKB-Pittsburgh, CKLW-Windsor, Ontario, WOWO-Ft. Wayne(Indiana), and WCFL-Chicago. I still liked WABC and WMCA from New York, but access to stations in faraway places provided me with insights about different communities throughout the United States. Often, stations in Chicago or Pittsburgh would play songs that never reached the charts in New York. Many small record labels in the Midwest and West signed local bands that had "regional hits" in their areas. Sometimes, lesser known bands received more airplay in the middle part of the country than where I lived. Songs like "Pushin' Too Hard" by the Seeds and "Hey Joe" by the Leaves were seldom, if ever, played by Cousin Brucie on WABC.

The Sixties youth culture was evolving. Many young people were no longer teeny-boppers, but they weren't quite flower children either. 1966 was part of a journey to a destination...my favorite year of the Sixties. Rock music was changing. The Folk Rock movement with bands like the Lovin' Spoonful, the Byrds, Simon and Garfunkel, and the Mamas and Papas was gaining in popularity, but once again The Beatles were in the vanguard. The release of The Beatles' "Rubber Soul" appealed to my intellect and emotions. Lyrically and musically, the "Rubber Soul" album was miles apart from "A Hard Day's Night". At the time, fans of The Beatles didn't know that most songs attributed to the team of Lennon and McCartney had been composed by John and Paul separately. The lead singer was usually the composer.

Beginning with "Help" and "In My Life", the songs by John Lennon were becoming more personal and introspective. "Nowhere Man", The Beatles' new US single in February 1966, reminded me of a nursery rhyme. However, the words were darker in contrast. On "Nowhere Man" Lennon sang about alienation in modern life. His lyrics spoke disapprovingly about a "Nowhere Man" who avoided people, kept to himself and had no worthwhile thoughts or ambitions. However, John didn't consider himself above reproach. He included himself in comparison to the "Nowhere Man" when he posed the question, "Isn't he a bit like you and me?"

In "Nowhere Man" and subsequent songs, Lennon didn't speak down to his audience or lecture them. Instead, he revealed his private feelings and failings in song. The admission of his own frailties, within society's larger problems, caused many people to think "John Lennon wrote that song for me."

So strong was the identification, that a bond developed between composer and fans. As time went on, John displayed a willingness to grow. So did his admirers. The mainstream media didn't get it. As Lennon became involved with new ideas and activities, his detractors labeled him a dilettante...but he was just being honest in his pursuits. It was his sincerity that fans treasured most about him.

When I saw The Beatles perform at Shea Stadium for the second time on August 23, 1966, "Nowhere Man" was their most memorable song. As I sat in Field Level Box 227E, Lennon's lead vocal was clear and crisp because of my closeness to the stage, an improved sound system, and less screaming due to more males in the audience than the year before. For a few fleeting moments, it felt like John was singing directly to me. On that hot Tuesday night in Flushing NY, just two days after I attained age 16, my lifelong identification with the moods and messages of his songs began.

In late May 1966, I bought another small disk with a big hole in the middle, surrounded by the familiar orange and yellow swirl of the Capitol Records logo. "Paperback Writer" and its "B" side, "Rain", were also radical departures from standard Rock love songs. In fact, neither tune was about "moon, June or spoon." "Paperback Writer", with a lead vocal and an unforgettable bass line by Paul McCartney, was a tale of desperation. Sung in a whiny voice, it was a plea for someone...anyone...to read a writer's manuscript. This was Paul's comment on people selling out in order to get ahead. The writer in the song would do anything...add more pages or change the plot...just to get his book published.

"Rain" was a song about appearances. John Lennon made the observation that everything looked the same whether it rained or shined. It all depended upon each person's perception...his or her state of mind. After listening to those lyrics for awhile, I understood for the first time that people often exist on different levels of reality from others. "Rain" switched on a light inside my brain..."Ah ha, I get it"... two people could look out the same window, water falling from the sky, and yet to one of them it might be a wonderful day, and to the other...damn rain. It was based on each person's individual experience and understanding, whether they saw life as negative or positive...the proverbial half-full/half-empty glass...and how they viewed their place in the universe.

Still, there was some confusion. Who were "they" in the lyrics of "Rain?" Many thought that Lennon was referring to people who were apathetic and didn't take responsibility for their actions. However, I interpreted "they" to be the generals and political leaders who sent young boys off to their deaths in battle while "they" sat in the rear lines sipping lemonade and congratulating themselves. When the "rain" came near them, they ran away and took cover, never getting wet. The dreamy, thought-provoking tone of John's voice, snippets of backwards lyrics, and the steady martial beat of Ringo Starr's drumming caused me to view songs and lyrics in a whole new way. This was music for the mind, not the feet.

The song "Rain" was partially responsible for me committing a minor, yet uncharacteristic, act of defiance during the spring of 1966. I always hated school. I always wanted to be somewhere else. One morning, the lyrics of "Rain" were circulating in my head when the bus dropped me off at high school. It was too nice of a day to put up with the same old authoritarian classroom crap with teachers trying to mold me into an image of who they thought I should be. I walked out...literally... four miles from Danbury High School on Clapboard Ridge Rd to my house on Putnam Drive.

I didn't have any agenda that day...no manifesto. No government was overthrown. However, I had an innate sense that I was being lied to...that teachers and "those in charge" weren't being truthful. Granted, that most teenagers go through some form of resistance to authority, but this was something more. For the first time in my life, I said to power, "You can't make me do this today."

It was just my state of mind.

CHAPTER FOURTEEN---Set On Freedom

I was never much of an athlete. My sports abilities were quite laughable. Yet in 1966, I was pretty fit. The surge in height during that year helped to even out the baby fat. During the winter months we played volleyball twice a week in gym class and I became a fairly decent player. Around that same time my facial hair started to grow coarse and heavy. I had to shave every day. Testosterone and muscle tone were flowing throughout my body. And, I had a role model. He was a sports star, but he was so much more.

In my life there have been few heroes, but I had one in 1966. Fifty years later, he is still my hero...Muhammad Ali. Just as The Beatles transcended music, Muhammad Ali was bigger...more important...than boxing. I first became acquainted with the young boxer, Cassius Clay, in late 1963. He was brash, showy, loud, proud and arrogant. He had the nerve to predict which round he'd knock out his opponent and he was always right. He wrote poetry, taunted the press, and made outrageous claims about his boxing prowess, but matched the talk with the walk every time he stepped into the ring. He was what I wanted to be...a guy who said what he was going to do and did it.

After The Beatles first visit to the United States in February 1964, young Cassius Clay beat Sonny Liston and became the Heavyweight Boxing Champion of the world. Then, Clay announced that he had joined the Nation of Islam...known as the Black Muslims. I had no idea what a Black Muslim was. However, many white people were upset by this revelation. There was even talk of boxing officials taking away his heavyweight title. That concerned me more than what religion he practiced.

I watched Muhammad Ali defend his championship as often as I could, including five times in 1966. There was no agony of defeat for Ali. I saw it all on "ABC's Wide World Of Sports" from George Chuvalo to Karl Mildenberger. However, I wasn't really a boxing fan. My interest in the sport during the Sixties was embodied in Muhammad Ali. As time went by, he showed that he was more than a palooka. He became the peoples' champion and used his position to advance various causes. Ali influenced others to rethink their positions on civil rights and the war in Vietnam.

It all began with one proclamation in February 1966:

"I ain't got no quarrel with the Viet Cong."

The moment those words left his lips, Ali's world turned upside down. He spoke out against the war, citing his Muslim religion, and stating his belief that the United States should not be attacking a third world country embroiled in its own civil war. Organizations, such as the American Legion, began to accost him verbally, saying that Ali was unpatriotic. Bigots called for him to be stripped of his boxing championship title and inducted into the army. Eventually, Ali received his draft notice, but he refused to step over the line for induction. Pro boxing banned him from the sport he loved. He was suspended from age 25 until age 28...prime years for a boxer.

Muhammad Ali symbolized the growing antiwar sentiment among African-Americans, including Dr. Martin Luther King Jr. My admiration for the Champ increased when he stood up for his principles. His personal sacrifice in defense of his beliefs left an immense impression upon me.

Having a black man as a hero was part of a slow change for a white teenage boy from lower middle class America, where belief in racial stereotypes flourished. I grew up with racism, but it wasn't the virulent, aggressive "Bull Connor" type with open hostility towards African-Americans. It was a "quiet racism", not spoken about often, but the message was still conveyed effectively. Some of the beliefs contained within quiet racism were that African-Americans had no concept of family life, no loyalty, no love between husband and wife, or parent and child. The harsher beliefs of quiet racism were that all African-Americans were natural criminals, lazy, stupid and incapable of having professional careers. As a boy, I believed those racial statements despite something inside of me that wanted to argue against them. Unfortunately, when a child is surrounded by prejudice, his heart may object, but the desire for conformity and the impact of peer pressure rules.

The irony was that most of the adults I knew were good and decent people, who would never hurt or harm anyone of color, however the inability to accept others as their equals...as human beings just like them...was their great stumbling block. It was all they knew...all they had ever been taught. It took a very courageous soul from the older generation to question the belief system of racism, but it took near sainthood to prevent the disease of quiet racism from trickling down to children. And from that, I was not immune.

However, being the son of an Italian Catholic and Eastern European Jew prevented me from taking a permanent step down the muddy path of intolerance. Occasional experiences of religious and ethnic prejudice directed towards me were always in the back of my mind and kept me from out-and-out racism.   However, there was one incident from early childhood that remains a source of shame for me despite my ignorance at the time.

When I was about six years old, there was a West Indian black couple living in the privately owned home located beyond my back yard fence on Putnam Drive in Danbury. Every now and then, a young girl, who was either their niece or granddaughter, came to visit them for a few days. She and I played together.   During one of her visits, an older neighborhood boy told me that I was playing with a "nigger." Of course, he said it in a hushed tone...after all, this was quiet racism. I had never heard the word before and didn't know what it meant.   The kid told me that the word was the same as calling someone a "colored person" (a more familiar term). I didn't realize that the word, "nigger", was an insult. When the boy told me to call the girl a "nigger", I did.

I can still see the reaction on her face. A happy smiling child was reduced to a frown with downcast eyes and tears in an instant. She looked away from me and ran off to play with the girl next door. That's when I knew that "nigger" was a hateful and hurtful word. She never spoke or played with me again.

In the mid-1960s, African-Americans comprised less than 5% of the Danbury High School student body. This changed dramatically in the 1970s, as new industries, like Union Carbide, opened up in Danbury attracting more people to the area. However, when I was a student at the high school from 1964-1968, African-Americans were a minority within a total student population of approximately 2,000. Yet, quiet racism lurked behind the scenes.

Late in 1966, during the first half of my Junior year at DHS, the entire student body watched a movie in the auditorium. The film, which was about African-Americans from all walks of life throughout US History, was sponsored by the local chapter of the NAACP and received the blessings of the school administration and school board. This was quite a change from another situation when one reactionary Board of Education member wanted an African-American teacher, James Caesar, removed from the faculty because the instructor had a goatee.

The film, "Got My Mind Set On Freedom", received its name from the title of a popular Civil Rights era song. Throughout the viewing of the film, my peers and I learned about many African-American men and women from various professions...lawyers, doctors, actors, cowboys, scientists, soldiers and inventors...all of whom remained in obscurity. I wondered why these unsung heroes never received any write-ups in the history books I studied. The movie piqued my curiosity about other historical African-Americans.

Later that afternoon, while waiting outside school for my bus ride home, I had a conversation about the film with a much respected teacher. I expected him to praise the movie. Instead, he looked slowly around the groups of kids standing near us, and in a quiet voice said,

"That film was mostly bullshit and propaganda...just to calm down any racial tensions that might exist in the school...there weren't that many skilled or famous blacks in American History."

His remarks hit me hard. Here was a teacher who I liked, admired, got along with well, and he said the film was a pack of lies. He spoke one way while in the classroom, but once school was out, it was a different story. Checking around the kids waiting for their bus, he made sure no black students could overhear him as he burst my bubble. Quiet racism continued to mess up my mind.

A little over a year later, when I was in my Senior year, Martin Luther King Jr. was assassinated in Memphis. My reaction to his death was mixed. I didn't really know that much about him except what I saw on TV. My parents had never discussed him much. I knew he was a man of non-violence, who was beloved by millions, but I didn't become well acquainted with what the man taught or understand what his legacy meant until I was in college. I was saddened by his death, but I also feared that there would be great social upheaval and rioting in the wake of his murder.

King was killed on a Sunday. The next day, Monday, we were back at school. In a first for Danbury High School, several African-American students asked if they could remain in the cafeteria throughout the morning, talk to one another about what happened, and work through their grief. To their credit, the school administration allowed these students to meet. I don't remember how many students attended, and don't know if any white students joined them, but I recall feeling that this meeting of solidarity in grief was a good thing.

Two months later, only a couple of weeks before my high school graduation, Senator Robert Kennedy was killed in Los Angeles as he sought the 1968 Democratic nomination for president. The next day was a school day. I was going to my first period class when I passed by two teachers in the hallway outside my classroom door. One of them, looking around the hall to make sure he wouldn't be overhead, but not caring that

I was listening, said with a sneer to the other teacher, "Gee, now that Bobby is dead, maybe they'll let the white kids meet in the cafeteria." Then, he winked at his colleague.

My 17 yr old mind reacted with disbelief at the cynical "joke". I was no seasoned astute observer of race relations. I was just a boy with a budding awareness of politics and societal changes, but I knew that remark for what it was...a racist comparison between the killing of a great spiritual leader, who helped bring about freedom to Black America, and the murder of an aspiring politician who appealed to many Americans, regardless of race and ethnicity. His remark rendered the death of two human beings into nothing more than a spitting contest...the implication being that white students needed "equal time"....as if the gathering of black students in the cafeteria two months earlier was nothing more than an extracurricular club meeting. This "joke" of his encouraged resentment towards a minority asserting themselves, and demanding the rights they were due, while conveying the false idea that the minority was asking for too much. I would encounter other types of racist "humor" as the years went by, but that statement caused me to lose respect for the teacher who said it that day in June of 1968, and made me wary of other utterances by those who would teach me.

In the early 1980s, African-American comedian, Eddie Murphy, disguised himself as a white man in a filmed skit on NBC's "Saturday Night Live". In the routine, Eddie powders his skin, dons nerdy glasses, and wears a blond wig to blend in with the white world. He walks into a store and picks up a newspaper. As he starts to reach in his pocket for some change to pay for it, the clerk stops him and says the newspaper is free. Boarding a city bus, all is normal until the lone black passenger leaves. Then, the bus load of white people starts to dance and party while drinks and hors d'oeuvres are passed around. When Murphy goes to a bank, a black employee refuses Eddie's request for a loan. Soon, a white loan officer instructs the black employee to leave the room, then tells Murphy that his lack of collateral is no obstacle...the loan is approved, and doesn't need to be paid back because Eddie is white. Wherever Eddie's character goes for the rest of the day, as soon as there aren't any African-Americans around, he gets all kinds of goodies for free...simply because he's white. Although Eddie Murphy's situation is an amusing exaggeration, it contains an element of truth about the advantages that Americans with white skin have over Americans who don't.

Quiet racism also waits for blacks to leave the scene, but it's not as funny as Murphy's skit. Open the door to a large office building and hold it for an African-American man to enter. Once he's gone, the white man holding the door turns to his companion and says, "They all smell bad, don't they?" A middle-aged white couple walks by a black woman with a baby in her arms, and a toddler in tow. They nod and smile at her. As soon as she is out of earshot they give each other a knowing look. The husband says, "All they know how to do is have babies and collect welfare." Two white teenagers drive by an African-American teen and wave at him cautiously. One asks, "Doesn't that kid go to our school?" The other replies, "Who knows...they all look alike."

By the late 1960s, I wanted to see that there was no difference between white and black. Oddly enough, it was another sport that paved the way for me.

I've been a big New York Mets fan since the team's inception in 1962. I was in college when the Mets won their first World Series in 1969. I missed only a handful of games on TV that 1969 season...even games from the West Coast. I went to one game at Shea Stadium in August, right before the Mets began their winning streak, which eventually led them to the National League pennant and their first World Series win.

There were several African-American players on the Mets. Two of my favorite players on the club were Tommie Agee and Cleon Jones. I watched them get big hits and make huge defensive plays in the outfield all season. I saw them standing in the dugout or in the on deck circle. I watched them step up to the plate. I observed their facial expressions and mannerisms. I listened to them during interviews. Over the course of a six month season I thought to myself, what difference did it make what Agee's and Jones' skin color was? They were like everyone else who played baseball. Agee and Jones had dreams, aspirations, and problems just like white players. They loved and cared about their families, had bills to pay, stomachs to fill, smiled and laughed, got sick and had injuries. The realization that we were all the same registered deep within me. It didn't matter who was white or who was black. We were all inhabitants of the same planet. We were all human beings.

What now seems like a very basic and simple explanation was a major revelation for me in 1969. It got my mind set on freedom. Over the next several years, I read Black history, worked with African-Americans, studied Malcolm X, was in awe of Alex Haley's "Roots", admired George Jackson and

Angela Davis, and loved the words and ideas of Martin Luther King Jr.

Despite the election of an African-American to the presidency in 2008, quiet racism is still around in the 21st century. It's not like the physical violence as in the beating death of Emmett Till, the maiming of Rodney King, the vigilante murder of Trayvon Martin or the long list of police brutality against Black males in Ferguson, Baltimore and Cleveland. There aren't any high pressure fire hoses spraying down upon demonstrators in the streets...no burning crosses on the front lawn...but quiet racism is deadly nonetheless. Deadly, because of its insidious entry into the brain. Deadly, because it's accepted as "truth" by many. Deadly, because it excuses the inexcusable.

CHAPTER FIFTEEN--On The Write Track

Summer vacation lasted for only 70 days. In 1966, I didn't want the summer to end. Too young to get my working papers and not old enough to get my driver's license, I spent most days hanging out at the Danbury Town Park on Candlewood Lake. My girlfriend, "Cindy", and I would meet at the lake most week day mornings and stay until the afternoon. Both of us took the city bus to the lake, but boarded at different stops. I got on at Nejame's IGA grocery store across from the Carvel ice cream stand at the intersection of South St and Coalpit Hill Rd. Cindy caught the bus a mile or so farther down the line on Main Street. The song, "Bus Stop" (by the Hollies), came out that summer. The lyrics about a boy and girl who get together each day on a bus became the story of our summer together.

When we weren't at the lake, we got together on Main Street and made the rounds of the various stores and five-and-dime soda fountains. Sometimes, we met up with other friends. Occasionally, we rode our bikes to meet each other on Southern Boulevard near Immaculate Conception high school, not far from the Wooster Village section of Danbury. Often that summer, Cindy and I went to the movies at either the Palace or Empress Theater on Main St across from the intersection with West St. We hardly noticed what film was playing.

When one is young and "in-love", you tend to ignore imperfections or things that don't add up right about your relationships. Although I saw Cindy and spoke to her on the phone during the week, I had no contact with her at night or on the weekends when her parents were home. According to Cindy, her mother and father were very strict and didn't want her going out with boys. So, we had to keep a very low profile as boyfriend and girlfriend. Everyone else knew we were going out, but not Cindy's parents. The situation felt wrong to me, but I didn't know any better. Maybe this was normal for many teen couples, I thought. However, deep down inside I knew that during the week we were sneaking around on-the-sly from her parents.

My weekends that summer were lonely. Cindy told me that on most Sundays during the summer her parents took her to one of the beaches on Long Island Sound near Bridgeport. I fantasized about going there with Cindy and her folks, acknowledged as her boyfriend, and having a great time near the salt water. I asked her about me going to the beach with her family. At first, Cindy balked at the suggestion, but eventually she agreed to ask her parents if I could go with them the following Sunday. She promised to call on Saturday night and let me know for sure. Saturday night came and went without a phone call from Cindy.

More promises were made for the next five or six consecutive weekends, but no phone calls ever came. My parents thought I was crazy to stay close to the phone every Saturday night, waiting for Cindy to call. Each Monday morning, I asked her why she hadn't called. There was always an excuse...but no explanation. For all my emerging "worldliness" when it came to politics and my awareness of social issues, I was gullible and emotionally vulnerable when it came to affairs of the heart. I didn't really know what was going on. In all likelihood, Cindy never asked her parents to include me in the Sunday beach trip.

However, there was a bright side to my confusing romance. Since I didn't see Cindy on most nights and weekends that summer, it gave me time and opportunity to expand my mind and explore other interests. My personality and interests got a kick start in directions that have lasted all my life.

In 1966, I had a black and white TV in my bedroom that received 13 stations, most of them from New York City. I stayed up late at night watching whatever was on the tube...Johnny Carson, old movies, reruns, Mets baseball. However, what fascinated me most were two provocative interview shows hosted by Alan Burke and Joe Pyne. Their programs were syndicated to the independent stations in New York. I'm not sure I realized how right-of-center politically they were at the time, but I watched their shows as often as I could during that summer. They were crude, insulting, and confrontational, often getting into arguments with their guests and members of the audience as well. No topic was off the table or taboo for the Burke and Pyne programs. Shows about abortion, prostitution, the Vietnam War, UFOs, ESP...it was all there.

Chain-smoking Joe Pyne was the nastier of the two men. Despite my fascination with the program, I knew that Pyne was not significantly different from some of his crackpot guests. Alan Burke was wittier and more intelligent than Joe, but he also dispensed verbal cruelties to those who shared the stage with him. Both hosts showcased lunatic fringe ultra-conservative guests, the kind of politicians who comprise the Republican Party in the 21st century, but they also provided a forum for well intentioned people with different points of view...people who never were invited to prime time TV on the major networks. For example, I saw Allen Ginsberg for the first time when he appeared on "The Alan Burke Show". Also, Paul Krassner, editor of the left-wing Realist magazine.

The hottest topic that summer was the Warren Commission report on the assassination of John F Kennedy. The Commission concluded that on November 22, 1963, Lee Harvey Oswald was the sole assassin of John F. Kennedy. However, two recently published books were in sharp disagreement with those findings..."Rush To Judgment" by Mark Lane and "Whitewash" by Harold Weisberg. I read the latter book, and watched with fascination when Lane and Weisberg appeared on the Pyne and Burke programs and discussed their cases for conspiracy in the murder of the president.

The questioning of the official findings influenced many young people to question their government's explanations of events and practices. It set our minds to think outside the box, to question motivations and the realities of what was being reported. Although some of the "conspiracy" theories have been disproved, and many people have come to believe that the Warren Report's conclusion has merit, those theories gave permission for people to later question other issues, such as the truth about why the United States went to war in Vietnam, who was responsible for the deaths at Kent State in 1970, the impact of the Pentagon Papers, the investigation of Watergate, the details behind Iran/Contra, and the lies behind the invasion of Iraq.

I no longer believe parts of the various JFK assassination conspiracy plots. I don't believe that Oswald was totally innocent. However, the possibility that there had been a conspiracy was a touchstone for a healthy skepticism towards other government explanations. It was an "Ah Ha!" moment which has kept me informed ever since.

I was always an avid reader throughout my school years, but felt restricted by the narrow scope of what I was allowed to read. Students were not permitted to write reports about books not on the recommended list. Nevertheless, while still in junior high, I read "1984" and "To Kill A Mockingbird", and the oft-banned "The Catcher in the Rye". In High School, I managed to read such titles as "Seven Days In May", "Fahrenheit 451", "Up The Down Staircase", and most of Ian Fleming's "James Bond" novels.

During 1966, another book played a major role in shaping my thinking on a particular subject forever more. The book inspired a belief that took time for me to embrace completely, but one that has not wavered since. It was "In Cold Blood" by Truman Capote. Once I started it, I could not put the book down. I finished reading "In Cold Blood" in a few days.

Outwardly, it was a true crime story about the mass murder of a Midwest family by a pair of misfits. The criminals had been in trouble with the law for years, however the book was much more than Capote's detailed telling of the sheer violence and depravity of the murders. The author conducted extensive research into the backgrounds of all involved, both victims and perpetrators. It was one of the first books of its kind in that respect.

As I read the book, I identified with the murdered family, consisting of a mother, father, teenaged son and daughter...a composition like my family at the time. I reacted with horror to the slaughter of these people, done quite methodically and viciously. It was incomprehensible to me how human beings could do that to other human beings. Then something happened that I did not foresee. Capote presented details about the killers' lives...failures...relationships. Unexpectedly, I found myself feeling sorry for them. Capote's presentation of the "bad guys" as regular people, who were wronged by others, and made bad choices in response to their plight, took me to an unknown area of empathy. Although, he didn't portray them in a good light, I became sympathetic towards the killers, Dick and Perry. The reaction scared me.

Certainly, I didn't condone the murder of an entire family, but I was beginning to see their killers as victims too. My young formative mind wanted to reject the sorrow I felt for these cold-blooded murderers. After all, I wasn't supposed to have any feelings for them...and yet I did...especially when they were hanged by their necks until dead.

There was a part of me that believed the pair got exactly what they deserved. Yes, I told myself, an eye for an eye, a tooth for a tooth. Those men had to die. They had killed four innocent people and therefore they must be killed as well. But I couldn't understand why I felt both anger and sadness over their executions.

Slowly, the reason for my feelings hit me. I read the details of their imprisonment and about the long days and months they waited, always knowing in the forefront of their minds that they would be killed. This seemed cruel to me. I began to wonder whether their executions were a form of premeditated murder. They should be kept in prison forever so they can never murder anyone ever again, but how would executing them solve anything...wouldn't it be just as bad as the murders they committed? Is killing really an antidote for killing? Does killing those who kill lower our moral standards to their level? What kind of deterrent could that be?

These were foreign thoughts and conclusions for me. I was brought up to believe that if a man killed another man, he should have his life ended as well. Truman Capote's "In Cold Blood" made me realize that if life is sacred, and no one has the right to take life away, how could one excuse an execution? It took a few more years for me to be totally comfortable with the idea...and there were moments when I vacillated... but Capote's book set into motion my opposition to capital punishment.

Although my main objection to capital punishment is on moral grounds, I'm also shocked by the number of people who are wrongfully found guilty of murder and sentenced to death. The errors have happened enough to make even the most ardent supporter of the death penalty consider that the punishment must be stopped. Once someone executed is found later to be innocent, they can't be brought back to life.

My belief that the government does not have the right to kill someone for killing someone else has caused friction with people I meet and those I know. It never ceases to amaze me how angry some folks get when they find out that I'm against capital punishment. Their response is almost violent in nature, as if I've just said something bad about their mother. They act wounded and hurt, as if I'm a criminal.

The most irrational reaction was from a group of college students at Cornell University when I volunteered to be a prospective witness in a mock trial for their law school. I had no idea what type of case was going to be tried until they called me up to the witness stand. It was a mock murder trial and the first question they asked me was whether I could convict someone of murder if I knew they might be sentenced to death. When I answered negatively, both the student defense attorney and prosecutor froze. They didn't know what to do. They seemed incredulous that anyone could take that position. They began to question me about being against capital punishment, rewording the same question in different ways. For a few seconds, after what can best be described as badgering, I began to think that I was the one on trial. Eventually, they dismissed me from the mock jury pool (surprise surprise) and when I left they looked at me as if I had slithered out from under a rock.

One night in July 1966, while writing in my diary, I came upon an idea that excited me. I was feeling sorry for myself because I couldn't be with Cindy. It occurred to me that Cindy had no idea what I did or thought about most of the time when I wasn't with her. So, I decided to write her a long note. It began as a love letter, but after awhile I wrote things to make her laugh and think. I was unable to finish the note, so I continued to write it the following night. This developed into an ongoing endeavor culminating on Labor Day.

By the time school started in September, I had about 50 written pages on standard loose-leaf notebook paper. However, this wasn't your common, ordinary, garden variety love note...it was really a manuscript. Along with my daily observations, which often included a summary of our shared daily activities, I made up jokes, drew cartoons, told stories, and created connect-the-dots pictures, mazes and crossword puzzles. I let my imagination go wild. Because the length of the "note" was growing each day, I dubbed this written effort "My Short Novel".

On the first day of school, I presented "My Short Novel" to Cindy as a memento of our summer with (and without) each other. She loved it. I had dropped hints that I was working on something for her, but she never imagined it would be a written account of our times together plus other forms of entertainment. Cindy kept my written effort in her school locker. When we broke up at the end of the school year, I tried to get "My Short Novel" from her, but like a woman possessed she grabbed it from my hands and screamed, "You can't have that...it's mine!" I'd like to think that the longest note I ever wrote still exists and hasn't been part of a landfill for the past five decades.

Working on "My Short Novel" helped me to hone my writing skills. I liked being silly, but most of my school writing assignments were devoid of humor. "My Short Novel" gave me the opportunity to explore the absurd. It wasn't important if everyone didn't understand what I wrote as long as it made sense to me and a small circle of friends. Many of the notes I wrote to friends were a stream of non-sequiturs designed to make them laugh. I didn't take writing too seriously...it was just something I enjoyed.

That same year a very influential person entered my life. He changed my approach to writing during my late teens and 20s by his example. His name was Sid Mesibov.

Aunt Ruth, my mother's older sister, was a very attractive woman in her middle 40s when she met Sid. Ruth was quite an accomplished woman in fields and endeavors that only men had done before her. By the time she was 50, she learned how to fix fighter planes during World War II, owned her own Manhattan ad agency, rubbed elbows with the rich and famous of 50s New York, was a licensed pilot, practiced yoga and meditation, became a licensed Real Estate broker, and eventually a TV host for an interview program on Cable TV. She also had boyfriends and more than one husband along the way. Sid, a dozen years her senior, was husband number three.

One day in the fall of 1966, Ruth drove her Karmann Ghia convertible from Manhattan to visit us in Danbury. Her new boyfriend tagged along for the ride. At first he appeared sullen, almost humorless, but as more visits followed, this man became one of the funniest human beings in the whole world to me. Maybe it was the way he delivered a one-liner or made up puns as he went along...never laughing at his own jokes, but maintaining the same deadpan face throughout it all. That was Sid Mesibov. He was a natural-born comedian. A few years later, after marrying my Aunt Ruth, he became known to our family as "Uncle Sid", but I never called him that. He was always "Sid" to me.

The first of Sid's writings that I read were portions of the letters he sent to Ruth before they married. She let me read parts of them because she thought I might find them amusing. I was fascinated by what I saw. His letters were filled with both good and bad puns, wild tangential thoughts stated parenthetically, and much self-deprecating humor. Although I did not realize it then, Sid was writing inane letters to my aunt in the style of a Groucho Marx delivery...the way Groucho spoke in the movies.

Sid was from that new generation born during the first few years of the 20th century. He grew up in a very tough neighborhood...played in the streets of the Bronx. He never knew his mother. She died when he was an infant. He was raised by his father and grandmother. Sid was a smart kid, who eventually went to college...enrolled in pre-Med. Then came the stock market crash of 1929, and his path to becoming a doctor was blocked by a lack of money. For a diversion, he loved to go to vaudeville shows and especially the movies.

As a young man, Sid developed a talent for writing comedy, particularly one-liners with puns. He was entranced by the zany antics of the Marx Brothers. When he found out that the Brothers were looking for gag writers to help flesh out the scenes of their movies, he submitted a few lines. Some of the lines were used by Groucho in a couple of movies. Sid became a stringer for gags. The movie script-writers detailed a particular scene and asked for appropriate lines to fit the situation. I'm not sure how much he was paid, or if he was paid at all, but efforts from stringers like Sid did not gain them any name-credit on the film itself.

Sid didn't like to talk about himself, but I was able to obtain some of his lines that appeared in the Marx Brothers' movies. A couple them were part of the "elephant" puns wisecracked by Groucho's "Captain Spaulding" in "Animal Crackers". Here's one.

"I'm going elephant hunting in Alabama because in Alabama the tusks-are-looser." (Tuscaloosa).

Also a line from "A Night At The Opera" hotel scene.
The House Detective says to Groucho in the latter's single occupancy hotel room, "Oh so you live here by yourself...then why is your table set for four", Groucho replies, " Why that's nothing. My alarm clock is set for eight."

When I first met Sid, he was working in the publicity department of United Artists. He gave me a few photos from "A Hard Day's Night", which, unfortunately, I lost as the years went by. However, during most of the 1940s and 1950s, Sid worked in various capacities in public relations for a couple of movie studios in Hollywood and then the fledgling ABC-TV network back in New York. He told me that his most difficult job was driving Dean Martin and Jerry Lewis to various engagements on a movie publicity tour. Lewis' constant antics drove Sid nuts . While at ABC, Sid worked on publicity for "The Untouchables", "Maverick", and one of my favorites at the time, "Batman. But, his first love was writing, and he contributed to a few scripts for "The Untouchables" and "Maverick".

Sid adored the Marx Brothers. During the late 1940s and early 1950s when Groucho Marx tried for a solo career in the movies, Sid was one of his public relations men. He got to know Groucho quite well. That was the dream job of his lifetime. It was because of Sid that I became a Marx Brothers aficionado while in my early 20s. One by one, I saw all their movies and memorized their puns and dialogue. Knowing of Sid's part-time involvement with the Brothers increased my admiration for Groucho, Chico, Harpo, and sometimes Zeppo.

I was not alone in being a fan of the Marx Brothers in the early 1970s. Their movies, "Duck Soup" and "Horse Feathers" in particular, were very popular on college campuses. Groucho Marx, thanks to people like Dick Cavett and David Steinberg, came out of "retirement" to entertain a whole new audience.

The resurgent popularity of the Marx Brothers became evident to me one day in 1971 when Sid and Ruth drove from their country home outside of Ithaca, New York to our house in Danbury. We were all seated around the dining room table on Putnam Drive when we heard noises in the bushes outside the window. When we wondered aloud what was going on, my sister Sara told us that one of her boyfriend's pals was outside trying to get a peek at Sid. The guy was a heavy-duty Marx Brothers freak who found out that Sid was in town. He was in awe that someone who had actually written lines for Groucho was inside a home in little old Danbury. The kid was determined to make visual contact, but was so bashful that he wouldn't come into the house and meet Sid. Instead, he lurked outside our dining room window and stole quick glances inside. Once Sid knew what was going one, he became an instant ham and gave big toothy Groucho-like grins and waves to the star-struck guy.

Similar to the attitude displayed by the Marx Brothers on the silver screen, Sid disliked pompous stuffed-shirts who thought themselves better than most people. Anytime he had a chance to deflate the ego of an elitist in writing, he would. Sid paid homage to the average man and woman with a series of columns done over several years in the Ithaca Journal. The articles, under the name of "Sid's Folks", were profiles of people living in the Ithaca area. Sid stayed away from well-known names in the community. Instead, he chronicled the accomplishments and dreams of the man-and-woman-next-door. He was fascinated by folks who performed a job by day and had a particular hobby or talent of which they devoted the rest of their time. It was his way of showing the uniqueness of each individual.

Sid never lectured me or told me how to write, but I learned a lot from his writings, especially his weekly Ithaca

Journal humor column called "Oddly Enough." In my early 20s, I began to craft my writing carefully, using my words with more consideration. Although I tried to use word play before meeting Sid, my writing pattern was quite derivative of his writings. Over time, I developed my own style, but made a conscious effort to use Sid's humorous writing format in my letters and notes to friends. Some of my most liberating written efforts were done as letters to friends and coworkers. When I wrote letters to acquaintances during the 1970s, they were filled with sheer insanity peppered with jokes and puns. I cut out comic strips from the Sunday Funnies page and taped them on the front and backside of envelopes.

Sid believed that every writer had a talent that evolved in its own way. One time, while having a meal with him at Manos Diner, a well known 24 hr eatery in Ithaca, Sid had a conversation with our waitress. They had discussed her writing attempts during previous visits and he asked her how it was going. Although she had some ideas for stories, she was concerned about her ability in grammar and spelling. Sid responded:

"Don't worry about that now. If you've got something to say, put it down on paper no matter how it comes out. Later on you can smooth out the edges. The most important thing is this...if you think you're a writer...you are."

One morning, Sid shot an elephant in his pajamas.
How he got into Sid's pajamas, we'll never know.

Sid Mesibov, 1908 - 1995.

CHAPTER SIXTEEN---Love To Turn You On

One Sunday afternoon in May 1967, I took a walk down Deer Hill Avenue, an elegant older street with large homes, stately trees, well trimmed lawns, and magnificent driveways. The song, "Groovin'", by the Rascals, had just come out a few weeks earlier. As I walked along the shaded street with its blossoming flowers, I was also groovin'...surrendering to the moment, listening to the birds, waving hello to someone I knew, and smiling at a couple pushing their twins in a tandem stroller.

That scene was quiet different from my usual existence. In my daily life, I was one of two naïve teenagers going through the motions of a love slowly evaporating. My long time girlfriend, Cindy, and I were in the process of learning about ourselves as individuals and that often conflicted with us as a couple. We lacked the maturity and experience to make a lifelong commitment to one another, but told ourselves that we would be together forever. One day, the status quo fell apart.

In mid-May, Cindy made the announcement as I stood next to my locker on the second floor of "D" building at Danbury High School. She wanted to break up and go out with another guy. Despite our decaying relationship, it was a jolt from left field. I was shocked. I knew that Cindy had become friendly with a guy from one of her classes, but I never saw it coming. She gave me back my ID bracelet and quickly disappeared down the hallway. A bit numb, I walked to my homeroom for the start of the school day. I tried to communicate with her through mutual friends, but to no avail. That was it. We were history. Well...not quite.

A few days later, Cindy approached me, said she made a big mistake and asked if I could find it within my heart to take her back. I couldn't believe it. Here I was, just getting used to the idea of not being with her and now this overture. I still had feelings for her, so I searched my almost 17 year old heart and said, "Yes." Before I knew it, we were boyfriend and girlfriend once more.

We pretended that nothing bad happened between us, but my male ego had taken a significant hit from being dumped at my locker while people I knew watched and overheard every word she said. Although we were back together as a couple, our relationship wasn't as close as it had been. Things were happening too quickly. The opposite feelings of rejection and acceptance, flip-flopping as they did in such a short time, left me confused and vulnerable.

One afternoon, Cindy told me that her Friday evening class at the Danbury War Memorial in Rogers Park had been rescheduled to Thursday. For several months we met behind the War Memorial building on Friday nights. It was our secret rendezvous. Her parents weren't supposed to know that she was going out with me. In retrospect, I don't know why I tolerated sneaking around on her parents, but I was a teenage boy "in love" and accepted it all. Knowing she was going to class that Thursday evening, I asked her if we could meet at our favorite spot behind the War Memorial. After a slight hesitation, Cindy agreed.

It was June 1st. I arrived early that evening. There was a small footbridge that crossed the small creek between the Rogers Park ball field and the War Memorial parking lot. I walked over the bridge and then lurked between some parked cars. I knew it would give me a good view of Cindy's mother dropping her off at the front of the building. I continued to wait while daydreaming about how good it would feel to kiss Cindy. I looked at my watch. She was about five minutes late, but I wasn't worried. A few more minutes went by and I began to wonder if I had missed seeing her mother's car. So, I walked towards the back door of the building where Cindy usually came out to see me, but she wasn't there. So, I waited some more. What was taking her so long? Maybe her Mom had car trouble. But, in the back of my mind I knew that wasn't it. She was over 40 minutes late. The reality of the situation hit me...Marc, you were stood up.

Cindy never intended to be there. That's why she had that strange look on her face when I asked her if we could meet. She was somewhere with H-I-M. The truth hurt like a kick in the balls. How could she do this after she begged me to take her back? Dejected...head slumped...tail between my legs, I crossed over the little footbridge to begin a long walk back to my house on Putnam Drive at the other end of Rogers Park.

It was between 7:00 - 8:00, on an evening blessed with an extended view of the sun due to daylight savings time. And what a sun it was. I looked behind me and saw the bright orb shining like a gigantic orange in the western sky. However, my ears heard nothing. All was silent. Moments earlier there had been shouts from children on the nearby playground, tires screeching from cars traveling along South Street, and the crack of a bat hitting a ball in a nearby field, but now I couldn't hear anything, not even the beating of my heart. What was happening to me? My eyes searched for something familiar. Seconds earlier, I saw people walking along the park road, kids hanging upside down from monkey bars, and bicycles slowly coasting near the tennis courts. Now, there was no one in the entire park. Absolutely no one...except for me.

Confused, but not afraid, my line of vision drifted again towards the sun. It was pink and orange. Each ray looked like a laser beam until it made contact with the many Johnny Appleseed clouds. They reflected the brilliance of the sun. I was surrounded completely...awash in pink and orange. The celestial show continued without interruption as I gazed around the park. I was inside and outside of time, both an observer and a participant. Then, as quickly as it began, everything returned back to normal.

Suddenly, there were kids playing, people laughing, ball games in progress and the noise of nearby traffic. I could not explain what had happened, but it was peaceful. Although the wound inflicted by a love betrayed did not disappear, I was comforted by what I saw in the sky. My experience left me with a sense that something big was about to happen...a change was about to occur. And it did the next day.

In late May, all of the AM radio stations in New York City began playing cuts from The Beatles' new long-playing record, "Sgt. Pepper's Lonely Hearts Club Band." On the album, The Beatles pretended to be another band playing songs in a wide array of styles for a make-believe audience in an old English music hall. The music was crisp and clear. Each song blended into the next without any silence between the tracks. There were unusual instruments, orchestrations and new electronic sounds. The voices of John, Paul, George and Ringo were so sharp and distinct that anyone could tell which one was singing.

I was attracted to "Lucy In The Sky With Diamonds" with its surreal lyrics sung by John in a high-pitched childlike voice. My high school classmates followed the songs on the radio. A guy in my homeroom sang "Lovely Rita" in a thick English accent one morning before class began. My fellow students declared which song they liked the best and observed that The Beatles sounded completely different than they had three years earlier. However, the jury was still out on the album as a whole because there was one song that no radio station would play.

"A Day In The Life" was the last track on "Sgt. Pepper". It was an elusive song prior to the album's release. The Beatles' native England began the controversy when the BBC refused the song for airplay. They claimed that the lyrics promoted drug use due to the line, "I'd love to turn you on." However, radio listeners in America didn't know what the objectionable words were. We were told only that the song contained drug references.

I wondered how a song could be blacklisted. Did The Beatles sing, "Yeah man, take drugs...it's groovy"? There was a shroud of mystery about "A Day In The Life." It became "forbidden fruit" because the radio wouldn't play it. However, what intrigued me most was the universal praise for the song coming from those disk jockeys who heard it. They teased us with "wait until you hear it" predictions.

Friday, June 2, 1967 was the day after Cindy stood me up at the War Memorial building...the day after my "other worldly" experience in Rogers Park. It was the day that "Sgt. Pepper's Lonely Hearts Club Band" arrived for sale in the

United States. Unfortunately, it was also a school day. I counted my money before boarding the school bus that morning. I had four dollars. My plan was to stop at the "Record Fair" store on Main Street after school and purchase "Sgt. Pepper".

The album was my first stereo recording. Sara and I received a small "Zenith" stereo for Christmas, but we owned only "mono" albums. They were cheaper. It only cost $2.67 to buy a monaural album, but it cost a whole dollar more to buy the stereo version. $3.67 was a hefty amount to pay for an LP, but after all...it was The Beatles.

Finally, the school bell rang. I got on my bus and asked the driver to let me off on N. Main St. I walked a few blocks until I hit the main business district in Danbury. The "Record Fair" was a long and narrow store located on the same side of Main Street as Woolworth's. It was owned by a middle-aged guy who spoke in a thick New York City accent. At first, I couldn't find "Sgt. Pepper" right away and asked him where it was. Without looking up from his newspaper, he pointed over to a rack of albums and said, "It's over dere kid, doncha see it?"

The brilliant colors on the album cover hit me right in the eyes. At first, I didn't recognize anything. Then I saw John, Paul, George and Ringo wearing bright lime, blue, red, and pink military style suits. Standing behind them was a collage containing dozens of familiar and unfamiliar faces. I asked the store owner which of the "Sgt. Pepper" albums were in stereo. I couldn't believe it when he said, "All of 'em." In fact, he had no "mono" copies. I threw my $3.67 on the counter and took off.

A few doors down from the record store, I ran into my mother. She was on an errand for her boss and about to head back to her job as a bookkeeper at Matz Lumber on White Street. I hopped into her car. Mom didn't have time to drive me home, so she left me off at the entrance to Rogers Park near South St. I walked as fast as I could towards my house on Putnam Drive. I couldn't wait to get there and listen to my new record.

I let my 6 yr old cocker spaniel, Taffee, outside for awhile. Then let her back inside. I ran upstairs to the stereo. Sara wasn't home. I was all alone...just me and a black vinyl disk. I removed the cellophane wrapper from the album and gazed upon it in wonder. It was extraordinary. It was exquisite. The album jacket opened up inside to reveal the four smiling faces of the Fab Four with mustaches, replete in their colorful uniforms. The lyrics for each song were neatly printed on the back cover...one of the first times that The Beatles, or any Rock band, did that. However, that wasn't the end of the visual delights.

Opening up the "Sgt. Pepper" album for the first time was like joining a club where membership included treats, gifts and goodies. Inside the record jacket itself, next to the sleeve, there was a 12 square inch piece of colored cardboard containing pictures waiting to be cut out. The experience reminded me of when Sara and I were younger and Mom sent away for a special package from the "Mighty Mouse" cartoon show. One day, a large manila envelope arrived from CBS-TV. In it were all sorts of paper displays, fold-ins, and cut-outs of Mighty Mouse, Oil Can Harry, Heckle & Jeckle, Gandy Goose, and other TerryToon characters. We spent many hours playing with those cut-outs and toys.

Now, at age 16, I was staring at cardboard badges featuring the "Sgt. Pepper" logo, a picture of the fictitious "Pepper" himself, sergeant stripes and a stand-up picture of The Beatles with "Sgt. Pepper's Band" written across it. Within the large letters spelling out the "Pepper" name were tiny photos of women's faces. A magnifying glass revealed them to be subjects of a late 19th century camera.

There was so much for the eye to absorb...and I hadn't listened to the album yet. I took the LP and listened to Side 1. Then, flipped it over and placed Side 2 on the turntable. I had every intention of listening to the second side of the album from first song to last, but after playing "Within You Without You", I could stand it no longer. I had to hear "A Day In The Life". I lifted the needle off the record and put it on the groove of the final track. The lack of silence between the tracks made it difficult to figure out where one song ended and the next one began. When I tried to place the stylus at the beginning of "A Day In The Life", I heard the reprise of "Sgt. Pepper" instead. I let it flow.

I didn't have headphones, so I positioned the left speaker of the stereo on my bed, and the right speaker on a chair. I sat on the floor between each speaker, level with my ears. The reprise faded and "A Day In The Life" began with the strumming of a guitar. John Lennon's vocal was hypnotic. My ears were tuned to his every word as I followed the lyrics on the album cover. John's voice was plaintive and sad. It pained him to tell us about the man killed in the car crash and the apathy of the crowd. Intentional or not, the lyrics reflected society's increasing numbness to the daily body count from Vietnam.

The cacophonous middle of the song consisted of different instruments played in unison from the lowest note to the highest. As the crescendo swelled, I went into a trance. The music wafting through my ears took me further and further aloft when suddenly an alarm clock rang and Paul McCartney was telling me to get out of bed. All at once I was completely awake. However, once Paul sang the line about going "into a dream", I was mesmerized again by John's voice singing "Ahhhh" to the notes of a haunting melody. This time, I was connected by heart and soul to that sound. I was part of the song. No... that wasn't it...I WAS the song. I felt the sensation of leaving my body and being one with the sound emanating from the stereo speaker, particularly towards the end of the "Ahhhhs" when Lennon's voice cracked ever so slightly. A very peaceful feeling came over me. I was refreshed.

There was more going on during the afternoon of Friday, June 2, 1967 than the song. I had been connected to something bigger than myself, bigger than anyone. Was it God? Was it a higher power? I had no name for it. Something had washed through and cleansed me.

Lennon's vowel sound that he sang in "A Day In The Life" was a common universal symbol...a mantra if you will...and it took me on a ride to another level of consciousness. I sat quietly for a minute or so upon the conclusion of "A Day In The Life". I didn't understand what had just happened. In retrospect, I'm amazed that I wasn't scared. It all seemed natural. For the second time in as many days, I had been transported to another realm. My experience at sunset in Rogers Park and my first listen of "A Day In The Life" are linked forever in my memory.

"Sgt. Pepper's Lonely Hearts Club Band" became a rite of passage for an entire generation. One could walk down any street and catch snippets of "Getting Better", "Good Morning Good Morning", and "With A Little Help From My Friends" coming from many windows simultaneously. I can point to that day, June 2, 1967, and say that my first listen to "Sgt. Pepper" changed me...it affected my outlook and shifted me towards a different perspective on life.

However, as much as I loved and admired The Beatles, I knew that they were only messengers. They didn't have the "answers" to life's questions and didn't promise us any. They didn't preach to us or ask us to believe in them. They weren't "holier-than-thou." The Beatles provided us with the impetus and desire to look for answers...to search for truth. The Beatles were just like us...they were seekers who kept urging us to find out about ourselves as they engaged in the same pursuit.

The Beatles kept us centered with "Sgt. Pepper" as our soundtrack.

CHAPTER SEVENTEEN---Break On Through

Grandma Bella and her second husband, Grandpa Joe Halpern, lived at the Benjamin Franklin Hotel on W. 77th St and Broadway in Manhattan. Neither of them drove. Two or three times a year, Grandma would take the train from Grand Central Station to my home in Connecticut. My parents picked her up at the station in Danbury and she stayed for a week or two. Sometimes, Grandpa Joe, who worked at the hotel, joined Grandma during the last week of her visit. Occasionally, we drove to Manhattan to visit them for the day.

In late October 1967, we were with Grandma and Grandpa in their small apartment. I was 17 years old and grew bored with old people talk. Therefore, I went for a walk around the block on Broadway. My goal was to find a newsstand and buy a paper that I had heard about, but never read... the Village Voice.

The week before my trip to New York, an antiwar march occurred at the Pentagon in which demonstrators led by activist, Abbie Hoffman, and poet, Allan Ginsberg, tried to exorcise the building of its militaristic demons. The group attempted to levitate it. Based on my limited knowledge of the Village Voice, I thought there might be several articles about that event, perhaps by one of the newspaper's founders, Norman Mailer (the following year, I read his book , "Armies Of The Night" about the Pentagon march). I discovered a newsstand not far from my grandparents' hotel. It didn't take me long to find the current edition of the alternative weekly...and best of all, it was free. I spent the majority of the two hour ride back to Danbury with my head buried in its pages.

By the autumn of 1967, I was in a state of flux. Many changes had occurred in my outlook and interests. The now famous Summer of Love was a major influence upon me. I was captivated by the hippies who flocked to the Haight-Ashbury section of San Francisco, but confused by the media coverage. Newspapers and magazines were drawn to the colorful people who made up the burgeoning counterculture. All three major TV networks had "hippie" segments on their nightly news programs. They approached their coverage of the hippies with a mixture of amusement, bewilderment and often condemnation.

Many of the commentators and writers held an unconcealed contempt for the young people who came to the Haight. It became clear to me that most adults were uncomfortable with the hippies. All they saw was nudity and LSD, but the sensationalism of sex and drugs was just a convenient flash point for the media. Beneath their shock, real or exaggerated, was the fear of a widespread communal ethos. It was the spirit of cooperation and disdain for the Protestant work ethic that had the "establishment" in an uproar. The very idea of young people rejecting the materialism showered upon them since the end of World War II confused the older generations. They couldn't understand the hippie desire to escape those trappings, ditch the world of "9 to 5", pursue self-discovery and thumb their collective noses at capitalism.

"Damn it," reasoned the CEOs, "These hippies will lead our nation to one thing...COMMUNISM. And isn't that what the USA is fighting against in Vietnam?"

Many older Americans thought that hippies were unwitting accomplices in a sinister Communist plot to destroy the United States. In reality, it was a youth movement not relegated to the United States alone, but occurring in other Western countries as well. Yet, some of our citizens thought that the Soviet Union had indoctrinated young people with "Das Kapital" and sent them on a mission to overthrow the U.S. government. The same type of people are with us today still, but instead of believing that Commies are hiding under their beds, they trust the steady diet of lies fed to them daily by the likes of Rush Limbaugh and Fox News.

By late autumn of 1967, I became interested in the main spokespersons of the antiwar movement...from Tom Hayden to Mark Rudd to Abbie Hoffman to Jerry Rubin. Eventually, the Summer of Love evolved into a marriage between the hippie counterculture and the antiwar movement. Today, many think that people wearing long hair, living outside of mainstream society, and engaging in left-wing politics have always been one...but it wasn't that way. Prior to the mid-60s, leftist groups and organizations consisted of academically inclined individuals who took their views with them as they tried to work within mainstream politics. When the hippies and New Left merged, dogma flew out the window. It was replaced by street theatre, protest, and activism with very fine lines of separation.

The image of counterculture members and war protesters became integrated in my mind. They shared a distrust of our leaders' foreign and domestic policies and desired a more equitable and democratic balance between the haves and have-nots. Student antiwar leaders calling for the withdrawal of troops from Vietnam and the Yippies trying to levitate the

Pentagon weren't unrelated efforts. They were part of the same energy. Both were necessary.

Rock and Roll was another important part of the counterculture, antiwar protests and happenings. FM radio became its messenger. In earlier days, FM radio stations were the domain of classical music, jazz, and college programming. Rock music was scarce on the FM dial in New York City until 1966 when legendary deejay, Murray the K, became program director on WOR-FM.

Murray, joined by former WABC-AM jock, Scott Muni, started free-form radio, playing Rock album tracks. WOR-FM featured both well-known and obscure songs from major and minor Rock recording artists. Unfortunately, the free-form aspect of WOR-FM didn't last long. By the end of 1967, the station's owners changed the format to Top 40 and Oldies. Shortly after the change on WOR-FM, many of the station's disk jockeys, including Muni and John Rosko, found a home at WNEW-FM. Other stations, like WPLJ-FM (formerly WABC-FM) came on the air.

By late 1967, I was an avid listener to WNEW-FM. The new FM Rock stations were a radical departure from standard radio broadcasts on the AM dial. Gone were screaming jocks who talked through the beginnings and endings of songs. Gone were the omnipresent loud commercial ads. Although the term, "laid-back", wasn't in vogue quite yet, it describes perfectly the mood created by this new radio format. Each listener felt that the program was personalized. The disk jockeys spoke in even paced well modulated voices about the music, giving details about the performers, instruments used and writing credits. Long uninterrupted medleys of songs were played, often centered on a common theme. The dj was given absolute freedom to create the sound he or she wanted. And, the music wasn't limited to Rock. It was not unusual to hear different musical genres played back to back. FM radio became as much of an art form as the music it played.

"Disraeli Gears" by Cream, "Axis: Bold As Love" by the Jimi Hendrix Experience, and "Buffalo Springfield Again" by Buffalo Springfield were played often on my stereo turntable in late 1967. However, the Doors became my favorite Rock band in the immediate post-Sgt Pepper period. I listened to their self-titled debut album every day. By October 1967, I was playing their second album, "Strange Days". I read all I could about the Doors, especially lead singer, Jim Morrison, whose deep-voiced vocals became the signature of the band. There was something about that band. They were tight...lead guitar, organ, John Densmore's drums, and that borderline baritone voice of Morrison. They weren't from San Francisco like the Jefferson Airplane and other psychedelic bands. They were from Los Angeles and had that late-evening-at-the-club bluesy feel to their music. The guitar playing of Robbie Krieger and organ by Ray Manzarek produced the band's unique sounds. No other band was like them. The Doors and their music became a musical necessity for me.

Jim Morrison and I had one thing in common...we sang from the same stage. However, we didn't sing there at the same time. As a member of the Danbury High School chorus, I participated in several yearly programs on the school's auditorium stage. One night in October 1967, Jim and the Doors played before a packed house at that same venue. Where I sang the venerable "Dona Nobis Pacem", Jim sang the mournful "People Are Strange".

How did this happen? The Doors' performance was part of Western Connecticut State University's "Fall Weekend." Originally, the concert was scheduled to take place at the WestConn campus on White Street in downtown Danbury, but the college auditorium was undergoing construction. The high school auditorium was the only other large location available. Miraculously, the powers that be at Danbury High (the same ones who kicked my sister Sara out of school one day because she wore culottes) gave permission for the freaky L.A. band to play in its auditorium. They would later regret that decision

I went to the concert with Sara and other friends. We sat only two rows from the front, stage left. Robbie Krieger was in front of some speakers. Morrison was to Krieger's right, in the center of the stage. John Densmore on drums was behind Morrison, and Ray Manzarek sat at his electric organ, stage right. The audience was a mixture of kids from my high school and college students from WestConn. We were kind of ragged looking and they were dressed up a bit.

The concert was surreal. I couldn't believe that the Doors were actually there. I knew all their songs by heart, including the ones from the new "Strange Days" album. I recall the band performing "Moonlight Drive", "Crystal Ship", "People Are Strange", "Light My Fire", "Back Door Man" and the infamous "The End". At one point during the show, Jim Morrison jumped off the stage right in front of us. He looked much thinner and younger in person than he did in photos. On album covers he looked much older...sort of a beery, beefy-faced guy, but in person he looked like a kid...one of us...clad in his trademark black leather pants while he held onto the microphone as if it were alive.

Towards the end of "The End", Morrison got carried away by the passion of the song and bashed his microphone stand several times onto the stage. When an article about the concert appeared in the Danbury News-Times the next day, it contained one nugget about that. When Jim banged the microphone stand, he gouged a hole into the Danbury High School stage floor. The article reported that our high school principal, Patrick Murnane, was so outraged by the "damage" caused to the stage that he threatened to sue the band.

Once I heard about the gouged hole, I became a boy on a mission. I just had to see it for myself. When I arrived at school on Monday morning, the first thing I did was go on the stage. It was really no big deal...not really a hole at all, just some scuff marks and a slight indentation. I stood there for awhile in the same spot where Jim Morrison had stood. The Doors' "When The Music's Over" was an earworm playing inside my head as I looked out at the imaginary audience and proclaimed,

"We want the world and we want it NOW"

CHAPTER EIGHTEEN---Last Kiss

Her lips were hot and moist as she covered my face with kisses and played with the hair on the back of my neck with her fingers. Was this really happening? It felt so good, yet I was afraid.

"Why are you so nervous?" she asked.

Only two weeks after getting dumped by my long-term girlfriend, I was apprehensive about getting involved with someone new...but that's not why I was shaking like a leaf. She was older than me...but that's not why I was scared.

"What if we get caught?" I asked.

"Debbie" and I were in the middle of an impromptu make out session...in school no less. It was the last week before summer vacation at Danbury High School in June 1967. Several minutes earlier, we arrived at the chorus room and discovered that our music teacher wasn't there. A message written on the blackboard explained his absence and gave us permission to treat the period as a study hall. Well, it doesn't take an expert in adolescent psychology to figure out what teenagers do without an authority figure to watch over them, especially during the final week of the school year.

Here's a hint if you need one...they don't study.

Debbie was a senior. I had a "look, but don't expect to touch" policy when it came to older girls. It was an unwritten rule that senior girls always went out with boys their age or older. A senior girl paying attention to a lowly junior boy? Not likely. So, imagine the unbelievable ego boost I had when Debbie, who had been flirting with me in class for the past week, whispered in my ear that we should go somewhere more private. But where? We were in school. Then, we had the answer... let's go to the music practice room down the hall. It had a door that locked from the inside, no windows, and best of all, there were soundproof acoustical tiles on the walls.

Still, I felt conflicted. Was this wrong to do? Should I stay or should I go? Biology won the internal argument as we went inside the room and locked the door. I was still jittery. I kept imagining a teacher or worse yet, the principal discovering us in our seclusion. Then, I envisioned being dragged to the main office, Mom and Dad receiving an unexpected phone call, and the punishment I would receive at home and school. Debbie had nothing to lose. She was graduating in a few days, but I had my whole senior year ahead of me. What if this incident, dare I say it, went on my "Permanent Record"?

There is nothing more mysterious and unfathomable during one's high school days than the Permanent Record in which every bad deed you've ever done is written down to haunt you the rest of your life. Our teachers always warned us about the Permanent Record, although no one ever saw it. We imagined that the record was filed away in our personal folders in the guidance counselor's office, but it would always be available to anyone wanting information about you. Woe to the person whose Permanent Record is revealed. Be absent too many days at school and no prospective employer will hire you. Skip classes and no organization will want you as a member. Stay after school many times for detention and you are destined for prison. No one could escape the shadow cast by the Permanent Record. My God, I thought, if Debbie and I get caught alone in this room, I'll never get into college, have a job, or move from my parents' house. I'm doomed.

However, as lust would have it, Debbie and I survived unscathed, save for the knowing winks and giggles from our classmates when we opened the door to the outside world. However, no relationship developed from this encounter. A couple of phone calls and a meeting on Main Street took place, but that was it. She went away and then off to college. I stayed in Danbury and had a nice summer romance with a girl named Beverly. Then school started, as it always did, on the Wednesday after Labor Day. My senior year.

I was never very active in extra-curricular activities or athletics. I was never one for "school spirit" and yet I really loved my high school. It went back to Junior High at Main Street School in an old run-down building that had been the original Danbury High School before it moved to White St. I hated Main Street School...it felt like a jail. Most of the teachers were mean, boring and listless. However, by the time I entered high school in September 1964, Danbury High had moved from White Street to a new location north of the city on Clapboard Ridge Road. It was fresh, invigorating and full of freedom...the polar opposite of Main Street Junior High.

The Class of 1968 was the first one to graduate upon completion of all four years at the new DHS. We experienced the Sixties together within a large student body of over 2,000 teenagers. We bonded together on many different levels. Even today, the special relationship we had from 1964-1968 is still evident whenever we have our class reunions.

Danbury High School was huge. It was the largest high school outside of the Hartford area. When I arrived at school on that first day in 1964, I thought the place looked like a factory. The buildings were labeled, "A, B, C, D & E". "A" building contained the Music department, auditorium, and Shop/Mechanical classrooms, "B" housed the administrative offices and library, "C" consisted of the Business and Science classrooms, "D", the largest building, was where most students had homeroom, English, History, Math, and Language, and "E" building included the gym, phys. ed. dept., and driver's education.

All of the buildings were divided into four semi-autonomous units called "Houses." The Houses were numbered "1, 2, 3 & 4." Each had a "House Master", whose authority was similar to that of an assistant principal. The House Masters' offices and administrative staff (including guidance counselors) were on their respective floors of the four-story "D" building. House 1 was on the first floor, House 2 on the second, etc. I spent all four years of high school with the same homeroom teacher, Mr. Trocolla, in House 2, room D267. My locker was located just around the corner...#D114. If you ask me what I ate for dinner yesterday, there's a slight hesitation in my reply, but I can remember my high school locker number immediately...go figure.

My senior year, 1967-1968, was different than the previous three. Unlike most of my sophomore and junior years, I didn't have a girl friend. After being dumped at the end of my junior year, I became shy and quite wary of becoming involved with anyone. I withdrew a bit into myself, spending lots of time alone reading and listening to music. Although I wanted more freedom, I was upset that the carefree days of high school were becoming less and less. High school offered mobility and choices, but with regulation and guidance. I could fail without total destruction...someone always had my back. I wanted to go to college, but was nervous about the next level of freedom it offered...a freedom unchecked...a freedom with more responsibilities. The frightening idea of finishing high school and beginning the uncertainty of college was in the back of my mind.

I had fun in the hallways and cafeteria at DHS. My participation in a food fight during my sophomore year was unforgettable. Winning a scholastic award during my junior year was a highlight. Also, there was a teacher who had an impact upon me. Joe Pepin was my Algebra teacher during my senior year. He was also the Class of 1968's advisor. I had a long history of doing poorly in Math. I barely got through basic Algebra in my freshman year and miraculously passed Geometry as a sophomore. I flunked Algebra II during my junior year and had to take it over again. Fortunately, Mr. Pepin was my Algebra teacher the second time around. He was the first person who got through to me. He had great patience with us and carefully explained each step. It made absolute sense. Everything crystallized about Algebra in my brain. There it was...bam. It was like looking at a 3-D puzzle when the result pops out at you after staring through all the squiggles and lines. For that one shining moment during my last year of high school, Math became clear. The right teacher made all the difference.

I became more politically aware in 1968. I supported Eugene McCarthy for president and was happy when the success of his candidacy convinced LBJ not to seek a second term. The assassinations of Martin Luther King and Bobby Kennedy occurred during the last three months of my senior year. My classmates and I would be affected by those shootings for the rest of our lives. We were saddened once a week when the TV nightly news programs listed the names of those in the body count from Vietnam... sometimes there was a name we all knew. The class of 1968 had to mature quickly, but were we ready to leave childhood behind?

Many events occurred during the two weeks before graduation. There were parties, cook-outs and a class dinner at the Amber Room banquet hall near Candlewood Lake. I had a good time, enjoyed a lot of laughs, and drank a bit with friends as we drove "over the line" into Brewster and Putnam Lake in New York where the legal drinking age was 18. I loosened up quite a bit during those last couple of weeks. However, a slight sadness remained for what I was about to leave behind at Danbury High School, a place where 500 kids in the Class of 1968 had taken a journey together through a unique time.

June 20, 1968, Graduation Day. During the morning, our class practiced the ceremonial procession in the auditorium. That evening the actual event was set to take place on the football field. We received our caps and gowns and brought them home. In the intervening hours I got a haircut at Zoel's barber shop on Greenwood Avenue in nearby Bethel. Then, I went back to school and joined my classmates in the homeroom we shared for the past four years. Each senior homeroom marched to the field opposite the grandstand bleachers containing our families. We all took our seats. Our time had come.

My memory of the graduation ceremony is very dim. I don't remember much except climbing up the stairs of the stage to receive my diploma and then walking away with the entire class towards "E" building to return our caps and gowns. A fence separated us from our families and loved ones. I lost sight of my parents and sister along the way. My head turned sharply as I heard someone call out my name. It was Tony and Josephine Tartaglia, parents of my childhood friend, Tony Tartaglia. They had been like second parents to me during the early 1960s. I waved to them as I continued to walk away with the rest of the class.

Finally, we arrived inside the the gym where people checked off our names and took back our caps and gowns. Many of my classmates had removed the tassels from their caps to keep as souvenirs. I planned to do the same, but forgot in my haste to return the clothes. I started to rummage through the containers, trying to find my cap, when a soft voice said hello. It was a girl I knew. She was returning her cap and gown as well.

"Susie" and I had been casual friends throughout our high school years. When I told her what I was doing, she offered to help me search. We soon gave up trying to find my tassel among the dozens of caps in the return bins. Then I remembered that my parents were waiting for me, probably wondering what was taking me so long. I began to tell Susie that I had to go, when suddenly she put her arms around my neck and kissed me on the lips.

Although the kiss was brief, it was warm and wonderful. Unlike making out with Debbie in the music room one year earlier, Susie's kiss was tender and heartfelt. It contained four years worth of affection and memories. When it was over, we looked at each other for a few seconds, smiled but said nothing and left hurriedly to join our families.

Almost 50 years later, I still remember that last kiss. It was a good-bye to high school...a farewell to our Danbury youth...a sweet end to the world we knew.

CHAPTER NINETEEN---The Whole World Watched

What's not to like about the month of August? It's summer. School is out. People are on vacation. And oh yeah, it also happens to be the month of my birth. However, on August 21st 1968, on my 18th birthday, the news was grim. The Soviet Union invaded Czechoslovakia after that nation tried to reform its Communist government. Video footage of tanks rolling down the streets of Prague appeared on TV. Not long after that, armed forces took over the city of Chicago.

On the night of my birthday I went to the movies with a friend. After the show was over, I dropped off my friend at her house. On the drive home, I turned on the car radio and heard a new Beatles single, "Revolution", playing loud and bold. The sound of Lennon's guitar was gritty, distorted and really kicked ass (who said that The Beatles could no longer rock?) When "Revolution" was over, the disk jockey informed listeners that the "A" side of the new single was called "Hey Jude", a record lasting over 7 minutes in length. He said it would be played later in the hour, but I never heard it that night.

By August 26th, I was becoming frustrated because every time I listened to the radio, "Hey Jude" was never on. No matter what time of day it was, I missed it. However, I had a chore for that day. The Vietnam War was still going strong, but badly, for the United States. Every male at age 18 was required by law to register for the draft. As a full-time student, I qualified for a deferment from the draft, but still had to register or face criminal charges. So, on that last Monday in August, I drove to the Selective Service office on Elm Street in Danbury. They all looked like nice people just doing their jobs. It was hard to believe that their actions might result in the death of a young American soldier. I filled out a few forms, the secretary typed up a card for me, and it was over. That was it. The process of signing up for the draft was painless, even though the consequences of being drafted could be devastating.

On the drive home, I was feeling depressed over what I had done...potentially becoming fodder for the war machine I opposed. I switched on the radio to try and get those thoughts out of my mind. And then I heard it. I knew that the song was by The Beatles upon hearing the first few notes of Paul McCartney's vocal. I listened to "Hey Jude" for the first time and loved it instantly. It had such a great melody. I turned up the volume control of the radio and blasted the song for all to hear. As I approached my home on Putnam Drive, the music hadn't stopped. Something within me said to keep moving. Don't miss a single note, I kept telling myself. So I rode around the block a few times, arriving home just as the last chorus of "na na na, na na na na, na na na na, Hey Jude" ended. The joyous song that told me to "take a sad song and make it better" put me in a positive mood. I felt hopeful for the first time since registering for the draft that day. Yes, everything was gonna be OK. College was gonna be alright. Life was good. But, that feeling was short lived.

1968 was a presidential election year. Lyndon Johnson took himself out of contention with his surprise on-the-air announcement that he would not seek or accept another nomination to be president. This came on the heels of Senator

Eugene McCarthy's success with substantial votes in the New Hampshire primary. Less than a week later, Senator Robert Kennedy announced his candidacy. I liked McCarthy, who had a contingent of supporters in Danbury, but I resented Kennedy's intrusion. Kennedy waited for McCarthy to test the waters and then entered the presidential race once he knew it was safe.

By the time the 1968 Democratic National Convention began, Martin Luther King Jr. had been murdered in Memphis, Bobby Kennedy was dead, Vice President Hubert Humphrey was in the running, and McCarthy supporters were hoping their man would get the nomination. The divisions between the remaining candidates were distinct. Mayor Daley of Chicago, an old school Humphrey supporter, gathered massive police strength to contain anticipated antiwar protests outside the convention hall. By late August, the city was an armed military encampment.

There had been a week of protests in Chicago by various factions of the antiwar movement. The Yippies, led by Abbie Hoffman and Jerry Rubin, were there. So was SDS leader, Tom Hayden, pacifist David Dellinger, and members of the Black Panther Party. There had been confrontations with the police all week, but on the night of August 28th all hell broke loose. Later on, an investigative committee labeled what happened as a "police riot", and that's exactly what it was. The Chicago police went berserk and lashed out against kids, women, journalists, cameramen...anyone their nightsticks and tear gas canisters could reach. The TV cameras caught it all, switching back and forth between what was happening on the convention floor and in the streets. The observations by reporters were unanimous. There had been no threat by the protesters to warrant the savage attacks by the police.

I was so overcome by what I witnessed on TV, that I called my sister into the room to watch. Both of us, our eyes riveted upon the TV screen, saw cops chasing people all over the streets of Chicago. In utter futility, protesters tried to protect themselves while being hit with nightsticks. The TV cameras showed scenes of people with blood running down their faces. CBS anchor man, Walter Cronkite, was obviously distressed by the situation. Our senator from Connecticut, Abe Ribicoff, spoke from the podium inside the convention and told the delegates about what was happening outside in the streets. He said that the police were using "Gestapo tactics" against the demonstrators as he waved a finger in admonition towards Mayor Daley sitting in the Illinois delegation on the convention floor.

Sara was 16 years old. She had a look of disbelief on her face when she turned away from the horrific scenes on TV and asked, "How can this be happening in our country?" I had no answer for her. I was stunned. It was beyond comprehension how those beatings could be taking place in the streets of the USA. What the hell happened to the Constitution...the right to assemble, free speech, and to dissent from government policy? Our freedoms were under assault. The brute force used by the police in the streets of Chicago mirrored the occupation and suppression in Prague the week before. A spontaneous chant of "the whole world is watching" arose from the protesters in the streets outside the convention.

It didn't matter whether those in power were from Moscow or Chicago. The whole world watched them react the same way.

CHAPTER TWENTY---Commercial Free

When I was a kid, my mother's sister, Ruth, worked in advertising on Madison Avenue in New York City. Aunt Ruth's clients were clothing manufacturers. Arrow Shirts, Lady Arrow, and Hi-Line were among them. Ruth was a "feminist" before the word was invented. She had her own ad agency for awhile, quite a feat for a woman in the 1950s. In addition to taking her place in a man's world of business, my aunt was one of the few women with a pilot's license in the New York area. On many weekends during the early 60s, Ruth flew her Navion plane from Teterboro airport in New Jersey to the Danbury CT municipal airport and visited with our family. Once, she took us for a ride over our house.

During the mid-to-late 50s and early 60s, Ruth Shaw became well-known in the New York universe of print ads, radio commercials, and TV sponsorships. Her name was dropped occasionally into columns by newspaper writers like Walter Winchell whenever she rubbed elbows with many celebrities at places like Lindy's restaurant. Although she was married a total of three times, Ruth was a single woman back then. She dated one of the Brooklyn Dodgers and also a Daily News columnist.

I recall being quite impressed when Aunt Ruth met Lassie at a press party. As the story goes, Lassie's trainer, Rudd Weatherwax, was a guest at the party and he brought the famous TV dog with him. Lassie got bored and curled up on the floor in a corner of the room. Ruth, who was a fervent dog lover, felt sorry for the collie and went over to talk to her. My aunt gave Lassie a tasty hors d'oeuvre for which the dog was most grateful. She shook Ruth's hand with her paw and gave her a lick on the cheek.

However, Ruth's advertising career wasn't always glamorous or easy. There were long hours, many phone calls each day, internal office conflicts and schmoozing with clients. In the autumn of 1960, she managed to get a live modeling segment on NBC's Today Show. It consisted of a few children wearing some Hi-Line clothes. My parents knew about the show and allowed me to watch it before I went off to school for the day. Dave Garroway, the host of the Today Show, was interviewing the children when all of a sudden the kids began talking about the upcoming presidential election between Kennedy and Nixon. One child kept saying that he wanted Kennedy to win. Worried that the show might have to give equal time to Nixon, Garroway signaled his director to cut away to...what else...a commercial. Ruth, who was frantic when the child's utterances were broadcast from coast-to-coast, told us that she suspected the kid's parents put him up to it.

When Sara and I were teenagers, Ruth asked us for a list of teen slang words. She wanted to use them in a magazine advertisement. I remember writing down some words on a sheet of paper and thinking about how *boss* (one of the words on the list) it was. I don't know if Ruth ever used the words in an ad copy. We never heard about it again.

I loved my late aunt very much, but she was a typical ad executive. What seemed like the big new thing faded away quickly to make room for the next big thing. Ruth was good at what she did, but she was never politically astute...social consciousness was not part of her make-up. Although Ruth was into spirituality, Eastern mysticism, personal-growth and meditation years before the general public had interest, she didn't seem concerned with the downside of advertising...the part that treats everything and everyone as a commodity. In the cold world of advertising if a sales campaign sold the product...that was important...not the product itself or the effect it might have on peoples' lives and sensibilities.

I never gave much thought about advertising and commercials until I was in my teens. Up until then, TV commercials were silly and amusing with original composed jingles (not popular hit songs from the past as is the norm today) and the ads were often about products for which I had little interest. My first awakening to the damaging side of advertising came one year at Christmas. I read an article that decried commercialism during the holiday season. The core of the piece stressed that the giving of expensive gifts, and great expectation of receiving similarly priced presents, was becoming more important to people than the message of peace inherent with the birth of Jesus. Dollar values were usurping religious beliefs.

Despite my lack of Christian religious instruction, the significance of the article struck a chord within me. As strange as this may sound, what drove the point home for me was the Peanuts' TV special, "A Charlie Brown Christmas". The annual holiday Peanuts cartoon had aired for a couple of seasons in a row, but that year it really hit me. There was Charlie Brown bemoaning the commercialism of Christmas as exhibited by society, his friends and his dog, Snoopy. In utter exasperation, Charlie looks up to the sky and asks if anyone knows what Christmas is all about. His friend, Linus, with his security blanket , answers him in a spot-lighted soliloquy with words taken from the Gospel of Luke.

"And there were in the same country shepherds abiding in the field, keeping watch over their flock by night. And, lo, the angel of the Lord came upon them, and the glory of the Lord shone round about them: and they were sore afraid. And the angel said unto them, Fear not: for, behold, I bring you tidings of great joy, which shall be to all people. For unto you is born this day in the city of David a Savior, which is Christ the Lord. And this shall be a sign unto you; Ye shall find the babe wrapped in swaddling clothes, lying in a manger. And suddenly there was with the angel a multitude of the heavenly host praising God, and saying, Glory to God in the highest, and on earth peace and goodwill towards men.

...And that's what Christmas is all about, Charlie Brown."

After that, I resented the intrusiveness of commercials and advertising in everyday life. It was phony and deceitful. People were trying to trick me into buying something that I didn't need by exaggerating its importance. Madison Avenue was using psychology in an untoward manner, trying to convince me that I was inadequate without owning Product X. The approach was disrespectful. Why couldn't I be trusted to make a qualified decision on my own? I turned off the radio when there were too many commercials in a row. I wanted to hear my music, not ads for pimple cream. Ads became more apparent in one of my college courses

During my freshman year at WestConn in Danbury, I was an avid listener to FM Rock radio. This continued unabated throughout my college years and well into my 20s. Often, I wore my headphones late at night while tuning the radio from one station to another...usually stopping at WNEW or WPLJ from New York or WPLR in New Haven. One night during

Christmas break 1968, I was half asleep going back and forth through several stations when I came across an unfamiliar tune. The song was "The Endless Tunnel" by a San Francisco area band called Serpent Power. Although it was well over ten minutes in length, I couldn't stop listening to the singer's tale about a traveler on train asking "Mr. Conductor" where the train was taking him, while an eerie guitar and banjo played in the background.

When the music stopped there was silence. At least ten seconds went by before a deep-voiced disk jockey began to talk. He told the audience the name of the song and started to ramble in his speech, slowly at first, and then went off on a tangent. What the heck was I listening to? I looked at the number on the FM dial. It was smack dab in the middle, 99.5. The station was WBAI, and guess what...they didn't play commercials.

Thus began many years of listening to WBAI-FM, a listener sponsored radio station, bringing news and music to the New York City area without any sponsor objecting to the content. The person I encountered on-the-air that first night was Steve Post, a very funny man who had a late night program called "The Outside'. He did skits and nonsense, took phone calls from many strange people between Midnight and 4 AM on Saturday and Sunday nights (among them an obsessive-compulsive woman known as the "Enema Lady") and gave mock serious editorials. As time went on and antiwar demonstrations became more frequent, Steve had guests like Abbie Hoffman of the Yippies and Paul Krassner (editor of The Realist) on his show. I also listened to his colleague, Bob Fass, who many people consider the father of free-form radio.

When a major protest rally or demonstration was happening in New York or Washington DC, there were hours of coverage on WBAI. This was news not covered in detail by the major TV and radio networks. Also, the station aired shows about Women's Liberation and often programming for and about African-Americans. No one else in America was doing topical coverage like that. Why? Because major advertisers thought it was too controversial and advised radio stations to stay away from it.

WBAI belonged to the Pacifica Group which owned radio stations in Los Angeles and Houston (whose transmitter tower was later bombed by a right-wing hate group). The station had pledge drives a couple of times a year when listeners could donate money to help with finances. For a few years, I was a listener-supporter of the station. The idea that one could listen to a radio program without inane advertisements interrupting the flow of the show was a breath of fresh air. I thought it was the way radio and TV should be.

Steve Post inspired me. I made recordings of myself on a reel-to-reel tape recorder, doing a make-believe radio show, inventing characters (for which I made up voices) and mixing it all with songs and double-tracked sound effects. Around the same time, my college started a radio station. Up until that point, all of my fooling around with my tape recorder was just that...fooling around. I hadn't thought of actually working in radio itself, but when the school offered a broadcasting course the following semester, I signed up for it.

Less than a week into the course, an "uh-oh" feeling swept over me. Beginning with the first day of class, the instructor talked about one thing only...making a commercial. Nothing else about radio broadcasting seemed to matter to him. There were no discussions on how to broadcast, use microphones, or spin records on turntables. Nope, the entire purpose of that first week centered on how one made an advertisement for radio. I kept hoping that something would change, but then came our first assignment. It was to write a script for a commercial and then record it. I was disgusted. I wanted to be a person of integrity, not just a voice promoting consumerism. I realized that one would have to know how to read a commercial script to be on radio, but it seemed like the concentration was on advertising. I wanted to be a disc jockey playing records, not a pitch man. It was the only course I withdrew from during my four years of college.

When I was in high school, I heard people say that by the 21st century people would no longer have names, and only be known by a number. I laughed it off as the stuff of Science Fiction. However, those of us who came of age during the Sixties were considered mere numbers back then. We were branded with a particular name. We continue to use that name without understanding its true meaning. That name is "Baby Boomer".

An advertising researcher, Florence Skelly (Altman), dubbed an entire group of people as the "Baby Boom" generation. During the 1960s, Skelly and her associate, Daniel Yankelovich, developed techniques to target a market group of young people born during the years of 1946-1964 for the express purpose of selling them various products. Skelley and Yankelovich viewed these people only as potential consumers, not as individuals. Skelly labeled this group the "Baby Boomers" based solely on the "boom" (large) numbers of births that occurred during the 20 year period following the end of World War Two. Madison Avenue and the mass media picked up on the term immediately. By the mid-to-late 70s, the terms "Baby Boom", "Baby Boomers", and "Boomers" became household words. Today, people toss the name around as a badge of honor and not the hollow marketing tool it really is.

Generations are defined by what they did, what they shared or experienced in common. For example, there was the Roaring 20s generation and the World War II generation. "Baby Boomer" does not describe the generation it purports to represent. It is purely a demographic term and has no connection to the history, accomplishments, hopes, dreams and aspirations of the generation that grew up in the Sixties. In fact, the only thing it describes is the prolific procreations of the group's parents from the World War II generation. "Baby Boomer" has absolutely nothing to do with young people who experienced the events of the Sixties, anything they did, or the values they hold.

Also, the term "Baby Boomer" implies permanent immaturity (baby), and has the effect of infantilizing an entire generation in the minds of many people. In the late 1970s and early 1980s, an unholy trinity of Christian fundamentalists, right-wing reactionaries, and multi-national corporations joined forces against the advancements and progress made during the Sixties. They blamed most of the nation's ills on those who rejected their parents' values and who believed in the equality of all. And, they used the term "Baby Boomer" as a cynical pejorative to fuel the fire of their culture wars against America.

I find the label "Baby Boomer" to be offensive and degrading. I do not call myself a "Boomer." I am part of the

Sixties Generation (Sixties Gen). The members of Sixties Gen were born approximately from 1940-1960. They are the cultural, social, and political generation of Americans who came of age as teenagers or young adults during the Sixties.

The Sixties were an American cultural, social and political decade from approximately 1963/1964 until 1973/1974. This was the time period from Martin Luther King's "I Have A Dream" speech, the assassination of John F. Kennedy, and the advent of The Beatles until the Watergate hearings, the Arab Oil Embargo, and the resignation of Richard Nixon. This time period is not to be confused with the calendar decade of the 1960s, part of which is included within the Sixties.

My definitions above are not set in stone. I recognize that the years comprising the Sixties, and the age of those who are part of the Sixties Generation, might be seen as earlier or later by others. Also, some folks might prefer different names like "Woodstock Generation" or "Vietnam Generation", but I find "Sixties Generation" to be all encompassing. It includes that generation's widespread engagement in the social, cultural and political movements in which they participated and often determined their later lives, livelihoods and avocations.

Sixties experiences as diverse as Rock music, left-wing politics, environmental awareness, stopping war, waging peace, reversing racism, smoking marijuana, becoming a vegetarian, working to help the poor, thinking globally and acting locally touched the lives of millions of young people regardless of what their political or religious beliefs are today. We were influenced by the happenings and events of the Sixties one way or another...no one was left out.

We're not "Boomers". **We're Sixties Gen.**

CHAPTER TWENTY-ONE---I Owe It To Someone

Men in suits and ties, their eyes hidden by sunglasses, were jogging on Coalpit Hill Rd near the entrance to Putnam Drive. They set up road blocks and stopped cars trying to exit the street. Convinced of the motorists' good intentions, they allowed them to pass. The men barked one-syllable words into two-way radios while one of them stared at the street and suddenly looked away. The sparse parade of two limousines moved quickly towards the Danbury/Bethel town line...and then they were gone.

The well-dressed men were part of a Secret Service detail for First Lady Pat Nixon, who had traveled to Danbury to see the childhood home of her father, William Ryan. The house, once occupied by Ryan, was located at 31 Mansfield Street in the nearby town of Bethel, less than a half- mile from my front porch on Putnam Drive. We didn't receive advance notice that Mrs. Nixon was about to visit. Unfortunately, there was not enough time for me to make a sign or organize people to stand along the route and chant "Stop the War."

Richard Nixon rode into Washington DC in 1969 proclaiming that he had a secret plan to end the war in Vietnam. Shortly after he became president, it became obvious that Nixon had no plan, secret or otherwise. Instead of ending the war, he expanded it and caused more deaths and heartbreaks for both the Vietnamese and Americans.

I began my second year at Western Connecticut State University in the Fall of 1969. A couple of weeks into the new semester, I saw a notice posted on a bulletin board outside one of my classrooms. It announced the formation of a campus antiwar group and gave the date of the first meeting. This came at a good time for me. I was looking for a group at college who would bring activism to the Danbury community, inform them about the tragedy of the war, and what it was doing to our troops and the people of Vietnam. I decided to join.

I felt alone in my opposition to the war when I was back in high school. Certainly, there were students who were against the Vietnam War, but there was no organized group at Danbury High. Opinions and positions were changing. In 1969, many people in the Danbury area were turning against the war. Demonstrations in large cities like Washington DC and New York were necessary for the nation as a whole, but it was more important to me that the message reach the folks in my hometown. That's where I wanted to have an impact...in my community...the place where I grew up.

We called our fledgling antiwar group the Committee to End the War (C.E.W). Its first objective was to participate in the national Vietnam War Moratorium. The Moratorium effort was designed to encourage students and workers to take a day off from studies and jobs on the 15th of each month, hold rallies and teach-ins, and cooperate with civic and union groups for the sole purpose of spreading the truth about America's war against the Vietnamese. We wanted to explain why the war was wrong and show that both the USA and Vietnam were devastated by many years of fighting and bombing. Sentiment against the war was gaining momentum nationwide as the population began to realize that the Vietnamese were not our enemy and posed no threat to the United States. Thousands of lives were being lost for no justifiable reason. Each week, the major networks listed names of dead soldiers at the end of their nightly news programs. The somber announcements of their deaths served as a reminder. It was time to end this scourge upon humanity once and for all.

The C.E.W. consisted of both professors and students. However, out of all the participants, those with the most passion and purpose were Vietnam Vets. These were men who had seen the war first-hand and were now back home attending college. It was one thing to know the wrongness and absurdity of the Vietnam war on an intellectual and fact-based level, but it was quite another to hear a Vet talk about the carnage he witnessed, including the torching and burning of villages and the killing of innocent women and children. These Vets were the most active in the organization and the most anxious to end the war.

Today, there is a popular myth, born of right-wing reactionaries, that student demonstrators and Vietnam Vets didn't get along. This myth claims that all protesters followed returning soldiers everywhere in the USA, spat on them, and called them "baby-killers." In fact, if it hadn't been for the merger of students and Vets in demonstrations against the war, I doubt that mainstream America would have turned against the war in great numbers in the early 1970s. Vets protesting the war they had been forced to fight were a major influence on the population as a whole. We were comrades whether we fought for the Pentagon or tried to levitate it.

The C.E.W. held events during the week of the first Moratorium to draw attention to the observance on October 15th. A series of marches and teach-ins took place at different locations in Danbury. We were trying to measure public reaction against the war by talking to people who had never encountered an organized antiwar effort. It was decided to have a petition asking President Nixon to stop the war and withdraw all US troops. The goal was to gather as many names as possible for the next week. Although the petition drive was largely symbolic (we knew that Tricky Dick would ignore it), we used the platform to talk at length with members of the community. It was a stepping stone that many colleges used to link town and gown.

One day we met for a late afternoon rally in front of the War Memorial building located at the entrance of Rogers Park, not far from my home. Someone stood on the corner of South St and the park entrance holding a sign urging motorists to turn on their headlights if they were against the war. A surprisingly large number did that. However, there were also angry people who yelled "traitors" and "Commies" at us as they drove by.

On Saturday, October 11th, I spent most of the day working from a card table on the corner of Main St and Liberty St in downtown Danbury. We had petitions and literature to distribute, but mostly we spoke to people about why we were opposed to the war. Many listened, took our leaflets, and signed the petition while others walked by pretending not to notice us. I became connected to all those folks who took a few moments to speak with us. I was making a difference in Danbury for the first time in my life.

Although I was fervently against the war and dedicated to the Moratorium activities, there was a part of me thinking about something else that day...the 1969 World Series. I became a fan of the New York Mets when the team entered the National League in 1962. In 1969, I watched many Mets games on TV including those televised from the West Coast late at night. I knew the team and its talent inside and out. For my 19th birthday in August, my father and I went to Shea Stadium and saw my hero, Tom Seaver, defeat the San Francisco Giants. It was the only time I ever saw Giant's outfielder, Willie Mays, my favorite player of all time, in person as he did calisthenics in the outfield (Willie was not in the starting line-up that day). Miraculously, the once lowly Mets earned their way into the World Series against the Baltimore Orioles. I missed Game One that Saturday, October 11th, while talking to folks on Main Street. The Mets lost that first game, but went on to win the series. As much as the Mets weighed on my mind that day, I realized there were more important things in life than baseball. Stopping a war was high on that list.

Moratorium Day, Wednesday October 15th, began with a non-denominational prayer inside the college student union and ended on campus with a night-time rally in Berkshire Hall. During the day, we were assigned to various locations and urged Danburians to sign our petition. I worked with a group standing in front of the Bradlees department store on Route 6/Newtown Rd. The location was a strip mall and Bradlees was its main attraction. We set up our table on the sidewalk just to the left of the store entrance and spoke to customers and passersby for most of the day. Conversations ranged from those who cheered our resolve to those who disagreed with us. The tone from war supporters had been civil until a middle-aged man approached the table. One of the women in my group saw him coming and tried to warn us...apparently she knew him...but before she could get the words out, he stood in front of us and unleashed a torrent of wild accusations.   He told us that we were traitors, un-American, and if the commies weren't stopped in Vietnam, we would be fighting them right here in the USA.

One of the guys in the group tried to reason with him, but to no effect. He had a platform and wanted to use it. I heard his name whispered by someone and remembered that he was an elected official known for his extreme conservative views. After awhile the man left us and walked into the entrance way of Bradlees. Immediately, he came back outside. His face was red and contorted as he wagged his finger in our faces and spoke words I will never forget.

"I hope you all get drafted into the army, sent to Vietnam, and get killed there."

There it was...raw and unfettered, hanging in the air for a minute and then splat on the sidewalk for all to see...naked hypocrisy. At first, the twisted illogic of his statement was confusing, but then the meaning hit me. He was among those people from the World War II generation who were so angry at their "children" for opposing the war in Vietnam and not embracing a "my country right or wrong" belief, that death became a desirable "punishment."

Several months later, I was in Rogers Park again. I spent much of my childhood and teenage years there. It was a place where I played ball, rode my bike, and fell in and out of love. On that day in May, the sky caught my attention.   A canopy of cobalt blue swirled overhead with white puffy clouds drifting towards the horizon. The beautiful day almost made me forget why I was there...to plead and pray that the United States withdraw its troops from Southeast Asia.

Four days earlier, Richard Nixon announced to a stunned and war-weary American public that our nation's armed forces had invaded Cambodia. Suddenly, the war expanded from the "Vietnam War" to the "War in Southeast Asia". Perhaps, this had been Nixon's secret plan all along. The outrage caused by this military action increased antiwar protests in cities and on campuses across the country. Danbury was no exception.

In response to Nixon's invasion of Cambodia, The Committee to End the War marched from the WestConn campus on White Street to the War Memorial Building at Rogers Park. Some people sang John Lennon's "Give Peace A Chance" while others held signs denouncing the war. As we passed the Danbury Police headquarters, two squad cars following us along our route.

The march was going smoothly until we neared a car dealership with a very large American flag hanging over the sidewalk near the business entrance. A fellow marcher, just ahead of me, tapped the edge of the flag playfully with his index finger as he ducked his head to walk underneath it. A car salesman, standing outside the doorway of the auto showroom, thought the marcher was being disrespectful and began calling us every name in the book. For a few moments, he was ready to jump into our procession with his fists swinging. The patrol car pulled to the curb. The situation had the potential to develop into a very ugly scene. Fortunately, cooler heads prevailed and the rest of the march to Rogers Park continued without incident.

Once we arrived at the War Memorial, we were joined by Danbury High School students and other members of the community. The "Pledge Of Allegiance" was recited "with liberty and justice for some", speeches were made, and prayers were offered for the end of war and safe return of American soldiers. After the meeting was done, I walked to my house on the other side of the park. I felt secure as I walked over a large stone culvert bridge which was part of the road. My stone mason ancestors, Grandpa Campbell Catone and his father Great-Grandpa Dominick, built the bridge back in the 1930s as part of the New Deal's WPA projects.

I noticed the deep blue sky fading in the glare of the late afternoon sun. Once home, I switched on my TV to watch the Six O'clock News. That's when I first heard the reports about students murdered on the campus of Kent State University.

Jeffrey Miller, Allison Krause, William Schroeder, and Sandra Scheuer were shot and killed by Troop G of the Ohio National Guard. I was shocked, saddened, and angered by their deaths. A phrase began to circulate inside my head. This internal tape loop repeated the phrase...IT COULD HAVE BEEN ME...over and over. Certainly, the situation on the large Kent State campus was more tense and dangerous than the atmosphere on my small college campus in Danbury, but I felt a bond and kinship with the four slain students in Ohio nonetheless. They were exactly my age...19. Jeff and Allison were actively involved in the campus demonstrations at Kent. Jeff and Sandy knew each other and were friends. Sandy, who wanted to be a speech therapist, was walking to her next class when she was killed. Bill was an ROTC student. According to his mother, Bill was becoming skeptical about America's role in Vietnam. He had just completed a test in his ROTC "War Tactics" class when he decided to attend the afternoon rally on campus.

Jeff, Allison, Bill, and Sandy were among a scattered crowd in a parking lot 250-400 feet away from the National Guard. Troop G was moving up a hill, their backs to the students, when, without provocation and as if on command, they turned around, pointed their guns, and fired into the crowd for thirteen seconds. When the shooting stopped, four students were dead and nine were wounded. Dean Kahler was paralyzed for life when a bullet entered his spine. Years later, the Scranton Commission concluded that the gunfire from the Ohio National Guard was "unnecessary, unwarranted and inexcusable."

More recently, in 2007, Alan Canfora, one of those wounded on May 4th, acquired a tape made from a reel-to-reel recorder whose microphone had been placed on a building's ledge above Troop G. For years this tape was in the possession of the Yale University archives. On the tape, orders to the Guardsmen can be heard as "Right here...Get set...Point...Fire." This refutes the National Guard's decades long denial that any orders had been given to fire upon the dispersing crowd.

Jeff, Allison, Bill, and Sandy have come to symbolize young Americans exercising their right to disagree with their government's policies. For me, their deaths brought home the message that our country will tolerate protest, but only up to a point...interfere with the war machine and one risks death. On that day, I understood that the war had come home for good. It was no longer limited to American soldiers battling the Viet Cong, or planes bombing North Vietnam. U.S reactionaries wanted to stop their offspring at home...by any means necessary.

Several weeks later, my parents, uncle and I attended the graduation exercises at Danbury High School. My sister Sara was in the class of 1970. I knew many of the students in her class. My parents were proud to see their daughter, who received far better grades than their son ever did, graduate from high school on that June night.

Many speeches by school officials, class officers, the class valedictorian, and other Danbury notables were made. One of the speeches received my undivided attention. The speaker was that well-known official who had screamed at members of the C.E.W. on Moratorium Day eight months earlier. During the course of his speech to the graduating class, he took campus protests to task, depicting demonstrators as unworthy traitors and implying that Jeffrey Miller, Allison Krause, William Schroeder, and Sandra Scheuer got what they deserved. All of this was packaged as a warning from a stern "parent-like" figure, who had the interests and well-being of the Class of 1970 at heart as they entered their college years. But, I remembered what he had told me and other WestConn students outside of Bradlees on October 15, 1969, and knew that his "concern" was bullshit.

The evening went on, my sister and her classmates received their diplomas, much partying took place, but that phony speech was on the back-burner of my mind. I felt that I had to do something to let the people of Danbury know that someone they had elected to office, and who claimed to care about students in his speech, had told several college students less than a year earlier that they deserved to die because of their antiwar views. The intolerance and hypocrisy of it all needed to be exposed. But how?

I didn't have any connections to anyone. I was just a college student without any clout. However, there was one thing I knew how to do...or at least I thought I did...and that was to write. So, after a day of procrastination, I wrote a letter to the editor of the Danbury News-Times in which I detailed my disagreement with the tone and substance of the speech in question. At the end of the letter, I wrote about the October 1969 Moratorium Day, and that the speaker told me and others, "I hope you all get drafted into the army, sent to Vietnam, and get killed there."

I mailed the letter and waited nervously to see what happened. The next day, I received a phone call from the editor. He told me that he wanted to publish my letter. However, he had experienced difficulty from the speaker before in terms of alleged misquotes. The editor told me that if I could get another person to corroborate what had been said to the C.E.W. group, he would publish it. I said I could, but in reality I had my doubts.

It was the middle of summer vacation which made it difficult to track anyone down. Fortunately, after much thought, I remembered going to the house of one Moratorium worker who lived in nearby Brookfield. I looked up his last name in the phone book and saw it listed at the address I recalled. When I spoke to his parents, they promised to give him the message to call me. He called a couple of hours later from his place of employment. I explained the situation and asked him if he remembered the tirade we received that day in October, to which he replied, "Yes, it's hard to forget when someone wishes you dead." He called the News-Times editor and the letter was printed in the next edition.

The reaction to my letter was mixed. There were a few letters in support and against me that followed in the pages of the News-Times. People called to thank me for exposing the hypocrisy. I also received some nasty phone calls as well. I never heard from the man at the center of the controversy. All these decades later, it is not my intention in recalling these events to make him into some kind of monster. However, he was well known for dishing out criticism to his opponents...with my letter he was on the receiving end. His outburst on Moratorium day represented those who thought the United States was always right and that no one should question America's intentions. As we know, there are still people who feel that way today. Anyone remember the Bush/Cheney war in Iraq?

The experience of writing the letter taught me about the power of the pen. I had a talent for organizing my feelings into words about issues I cared about passionately. It also gave me the confidence and determination to continue that type of composition. For the next three years, I was an avid writer of letters to the editor of the Danbury News-Times, most having to do with the Vietnam War, politics, and popular culture.

Every year, on May 4th, I think about Jeff, Allison, Bill and Sandy and how they never had the chance to have adult lives and grow old with the rest of us. If they were alive today, each of the Kent State Four would be over 65 years old. I've always tried to honor their memories, both personally and politically.

As the David Crosby song goes:

"I feel like I owe it to someone."

CHAPTER TWENTY-TWO---We Forgot Billy Preston

On April 10, 1970, Paul McCartney made official what many people suspected...that The Beatles were no more. I heard the announcement during the evening news on WCBS-TV New York. The words came in a few sentences from news anchor Jim Jensen. Short, perfunctory, emotionless...that's all folks.

The break-up of The Beatles created a void in my life. I grew up with the band from age 13 to 20. I wasn't ready for them to quit. Damn...I wanted more. The following month, sick with a temperature of 101 degrees, I endured the movie, "Let It Be", at the Palace Theater in Danbury. Sad and lethargic, it was like watching your family disintegrate in front of you.

For the next year, I tried to fill the emptiness by obtaining bootleg recordings of Beatles concerts. Crude, uneven, and often unlistenable, my ears strained to hear the musical magic from the past 6 years. But, it wasn't there. I came to the conclusion that if I couldn't have The Beatles, I wanted to understand the music that influenced them. Musically, I went back to a time that I didn't remember very well...50s Rock 'n' Roll. Whenever I had some cash, I bought up old albums by early rockers like Chuck Berry, Little Richard, Carl Perkins, Buddy Holly, Sam Cook and various Doo-Wop groups. My interest coincided with listening to a local Doo-Wop tribute band from Danbury called "Guy and the Greasers." My sister's boyfriend played guitar. "Guy", the lead singer, did the songs justice. Years later, he gained fame as Ralph, the New York State Lottery TV spokesperson.

I still held on to the hope that The Beatles would get back together and all would be right with the world. Rumors flew from the pages of Rolling Stone magazine, but they never rang true. Music had always been like a drug to me. It made me happy...it consoled me when I was sad. The absence of new Beatles song opened my mind to other sources of joy. During the summer of 1970, marijuana entered my life.

One day, my friend Rob rolled a joint for us to smoke. We sat in his basement as he showed me how to inhale and hold the smoke in my lungs for awhile, then exhale. I was not a smoker. Occasionally, I bought a pack of cigarettes just to be cool. When the first toke of pot smoke entered my lungs, it burned. I coughed like crazy. Rob told me that no one got really high the first time they smoked. I'm not sure if that's true for everyone, but he was right in my case. I felt a slight buzz, but it wasn't until the next time that I got stoned. I liked it...I liked it a lot. Over the next decade, I smoked dope on a regular basis, almost daily during the first year or so. I enjoyed how my senses were heightened...time would stand still and then it would seem to speed up...music sounded fantastic...food tasted out of this world(munchies!)...sex was great.

During the Sixties, marijuana became a tribal ritual. I smoked it with friends and new acquaintances who soon became friends. It was a bond that united us...another common link for the Sixties Generation. We trusted one another. We grew it. We shared what we had. No one worried about getting cheated when they bought dope from a friend...no one thought that the pot they inhaled might be laced with anything harmful. I smoked at concerts, parties, and parks. I even took an English final exam while high, and passed it.

The amount of times I smoked declined as the 70s decade waned. By the late 70s, marijuana began to lose its luster. By the early 1980s, I found that it was getting harder to trust sellers and the weed itself was often mixed with stuff that gave me body aches and muscle spasms. It no longer felt like a shared experience. It wasn't fun anymore. After a dozen years of being in love with Mary Jane, I decided to stop. My heaviest smoking year was 1971, but I was totally straight when I attended the biggest concert of that year.

In late July, a story began circulating in the New York City media...George Harrison was organizing a benefit concert for the people of Bangladesh at the request of his friend, Ravi Shankar. The original name of the concert was "Harrison and Friends", but was changed to the "Concert for Bangladesh". At first, this musical event was scheduled for the evening of Saturday, July 31st, but based on anticipated ticket sales the concert became two performances on the afternoon and evening of Sunday, August 1st. There was much speculation about who the performers would be.

Not seeing the Concert for Bangladesh wasn't an option for me. I *had* to see it. However, in the days before Ticketron and Ticketmaster, when one had to line up in front of the ticket office window at the concert venue, I was at a severe disadvantage. The concert was in a few days at Madison Square Garden in New York and I was stuck in Danbury Connecticut without a ticket. My good friend, Gilberte Najamy, who was with me when I saw The Beatles at Shea Stadium, found a ticket agency in Stamford CT that still had a few remaining tickets. We were supposed to get two tickets for the both of us, but then Gilberte remembered that she had a work commitment the same day. Still, she accompanied me on the hour drive to the ticket agency in Stamford where I became acquainted with the term, "scalping". What I paid for my ticket to the Concert for Bangladesh was cheap by today's standards. However, the actual price was $7.50, and the ticket agency charged me $18.00...more than twice the cost. I didn't have much money in those days, but I handed over my cash, grabbed the ticket and waited for the big day to arrive.

My ticket, which had the original name of the concert and its old date of July 31st printed on it, was for the afternoon performance. Not owning a car in those days, I took a bus from Danbury to the Port Authority terminal in Manhattan and got a cab to Madison Square. By that Sunday, I knew who some of the performers would be...George Harrison, Ringo Starr, Eric Clapton, Klaus Voorman, Leon Russell, and Billy Preston. Earlier in the week, there had been talk about all four Beatles appearing on stage, but that rumor ended quickly. Still, there was faint hope that John Lennon might show up.

I hadn't been to many large concerts since seeing The Beatles in 1966. During my late high school and early college years, I saw the Doors, Grass Roots, Blues Magoos, Rare Earth in Danbury, the J. Geils Band and Yes in Waterbury, but the Concert for Bangladesh was the biggest concert I had attended in five years. Most of the people in the audience were close to my age of 21, a few younger people, and many folks in their late 20s and early 30s. The gathering was a cross-section of the New York City area with nearly an equal number of males and females in attendance as well as people of color, although there were more white faces than black.

I had an aisle seat in the Loge section, stage right and had a good view. I wore my 1971 "uniform" which consisted of a blue denim work shirt and bell-bottom jeans. I sat next to two girls around my age, both wore army jackets and jeans. We talked quite a bit in the beginning, but not much during the show. And then there was light, and it was shining down upon George Harrison as he introduced Ravi Shankar and his ensemble. Ravi knew the crowd had come to hear Harrison and his friends, but he asked us to listen to and absorb the more complex attributes of his Indian music. His portion of the show drew attention to the reason for the concert...to raise money for the ravaged people of Bangladesh. Although I listened respectfully to the Indian music, I was impatient for Rock 'n' Roll to take the stage.

After the Indian musicians finished, a crew set up microphones, and made their sound checks. The stage went dark for a few minutes. The lights came back on and the assembled band launched into George Harrison's "Wah-Wah". I never heard so many guitars and horns playing at once. The song sounded remarkably like it did on Harrison's "All Things Must Pass" album from the previous year...except much louder. It was a glorious introduction to the concert and the crowd was on its feet for the entire number. George and Company did two more songs in a row from that album, "My Sweet Lord" and "Awaiting On You All".

Harrison looked great in his white suit and orange shirt. His voice sounded strong, and the back-up singers, especially on "My Sweet Lord", added quite a punch to the songs. Eric Clapton maintained a low profile during the entire concert, sometimes standing with his back to the audience. Years later, we learned that he was in the midst of heroin addiction, and had been very ill before the start of the performance.

One of the things that made the concert so great was the diversity of music...Rock, Folk, Gospel, Soul, R&B...it was all there. Billy Preston, who could arguably be called the 5th Beatle, had the crowd rocking with his soulful tune, "That's The Way God Planned It". Towards the end of the song, he walked away from the organ and did a wild stomping dance in front of George, running back to his chair just in time to play the ending.

Unlike the frenzied Beatles concerts, where one had to struggle to hear the band, this concert was different. Technology had taken a giant leap during the previous five years, improving the sound of vocals and instruments. Girls weren't screaming non-stop. The crowd was noisy, but the band could be heard very well.

Then came Ringo's turn to sing. The familiar guitar hook from "It Don't Come Easy" was instantly recognizable. Again, the crowd rose to its feet. We were seeing two Beatles on stage together and hearing a song in which both of them had played on record. That was one of two moments during the concert in which I almost had to pinch myself to make sure I wasn't dreaming. Ringo's voice was a little shaky and he messed up the lyrics twice (during the line, "And this love of mine keeps growing all the time.") Was he nervous? Yes, he had to be.

Slowing down the pace, George sang the last of the afternoon's songs from "All Things Must Pass". A somber tune...a cautionary tale...telling us not to let sadness take over our lives, George's "Beware Of Darkness" again showed him in good voice with Leon Russell singing one of the verses. I always liked the song, but found it a bit maudlin. It wasn't until I saw the tribute "Concert for George" in 2003, and heard "Beware Of Darkness" performed by Eric Clapton, that I realized how much the song reminded me of George and how much I missed him. He was often criticized for "preaching" in some of his songs, but he was just sharing. Today, I can't listen to that song without getting a lump in my throat...the words ring true.

There hadn't been too many introductions to songs up until that point in the concert. Then George introduced the individual band members. I found this to be one of the more enjoyable parts of the show. George told us that people had "cancelled a few gigs" to be in the concert. Clapton, Voorman, and Russell received loud applause, but it was Ringo (the first to be introduced) who received a sustained ovation...ending with an impromptu organ snippet from "Yellow Submarine" played by Leon Russell. Anyone who has ever seen the concert film remembers George turning to the band and inquiring if he had forgotten to introduce anyone. After a few seconds, he announced, "We've forgotten Billy Preston." Billy was roundly cheered.

Shortly after the intros, without any announcement or fanfare, the assembled band played the beginning notes to a song which the audience knew right away, "While My Guitar Gently Weeps". This was the first of three Harrison songs performed during the course of the concert that George recorded with The Beatles. It was the only time I envisioned what the concert would have been like had John Lennon and Paul McCartney been on stage. George, Ringo, and Eric had been on the original White Album recording of "While My Guitar Gently Weeps". Therefore, it wasn't much of a stretch to imagine all four of The Beatles on stage. I was only 21 years old, and not given to public displays of emotion, but my eyes were wet during that number. I was not alone...people all around me had tears on their faces during the song. George sang the lines of one verse out of order, but no one cared. His voice sounded like it did when he sang the song on "The Beatles" White album.

As if to knock us out of our nostalgic stupor, George said into the microphone, "Here's another number from Leon", which heralded the hardest rocking songs of the concert. Leon Russell performed a medley of the Rolling Stones' "Jumpin' Jack Flash", and the oft-covered 50s rocker, "Young Blood" (originally done by the Coasters). What I remember most is the incessant tom-tom beat by Ringo Starr and Jim Keltner. The audience kept time with their stomping feet. The entire Loge section rocked in rhythm with the drums. I could feel the pulse-like pounding throughout my body. Leon's woeful sing-song tale of leaving his lover for a younger girl was the connection between the two songs. When he returned to "Jumpin' Jack Flash" at the end of the set, the vibration in the floor was even stronger than the first time. Many concert attendees cite Russell's performance as the best of that day.

I don't know how the set list for the concert was planned, but the acoustic version of "Here Comes The Sun", which Harrison and Pete Ham of Badfinger performed, was quite a counterpoint to Leon's raucous medley. Note for note, it was a perfect rendition of one of George's most acclaimed Beatles' tunes.

There was a lot of movement on stage as George leaned into his microphone and said matter-of-factly, "Here's a friend of all of us, Bob Dylan." I couldn't make out what he said at first, then I began hearing people near me say, "Oh my God, it's Dylan." Just when I thought the concert couldn't get any better...it did. When Dylan walked up to the microphone, it was a total surprise...the second time I thought about pinching myself. Was it real or was I dreaming?

Dylan sang "A Hard Rain's a-Gonna Fall", "It Takes A Lot To Laugh, It Takes A Train To Cry", "Blowin' In The Wind", and "Just Like A Woman I was quite impressed by the familiar antiwar favorite, "A Hard Rain's a-Gonna Fall". I knew "Blowin' In The Wind" by heart, learning it first in a Junior High music class. It was the only song during the concert in which I heard the audience sing along. However, my favorite from the Dylan set was "Just Like A Woman".

Standing side by side on "Just Like A Woman" was Ringo Starr, George Harrison, and Bob Dylan. There are times when one knows they are seeing history in the making. I told myself, "don't forget this moment...two of The Beatles and Dylan are on stage together...this might not ever happen again." And there it is still in my mind's eye...Ringo with tambourine in hand, George Harrison playing guitar and singing back-up vocals to Bob Dylan's lead. As quickly as he entered, Dylan walked off the stage and was gone.

My memory of the next song, "Something", is a bit fuzzy. I can't state this with absolute certainty, but "Something" may have been my "bathroom song" out of necessity. The concert had been going on for almost 3 hours, and I had a bus to catch back to Danbury. For the first time all day, I became a clock watcher. Fortunately, the encore song was next, the recently penned George Harrison song, "Bangladesh", in which he told us why he decided to put on the concert for the poverty stricken people of that war-torn nation.

I said a quick good-bye to the people sitting next to me, ran down the stairs, and made a hasty retreat to the streets outside. It was raining on that early Sunday evening and yet I was able to get a taxi right away. The driver asked me, "So, what's going on at the Garden today?" As I told him about the concert, he kept repeating, "Wow, you've got to be kidding me."

Although I wished for a Beatles reunion that day, I realize now that the Concert for Bangladesh was better off without their competitive egos and the legal rancor that existed among them at the time. What made The Concert for Bangladesh unique was its basic humanitarian purpose, the many artists who dedicated themselves to that worthy cause, the wide range of musical diversity, and a very appreciative audience who loved and respected it all.

I still have the ticket stub.

CHAPTER TWENTY-THREE---Not Selected...Not Elected

Danbury Connecticut was changing in the early 1970s, but not necessarily for the better. New industries began to arrive. The largest was Union Carbide. Although the corporation didn't complete its move until 1983, its initial announcement to leave New York influenced other big businesses to eye Danbury as their new home.

When I was growing up during the 50s and 60s, Danbury was a small city with some manufacturing and factories (it had been called "The Hat City" for decades), however once the large corporations arrived there was an onslaught of unbridled growth. Construction was going on all over the town. Condominiums began to sprout up everywhere...even in the most unlikely locations. Near my old neighborhood on the south side of town, condos were built into rocky ledges on Coalpit Hill Rd, on green areas near the Rogers Park Pond, and in the open fields behind my house on Putnam Drive...the same fields in which I played and dreamed during my youth.

I was still in college during the early 70s. In 1971, I was partying a lot, wasting my time in an unrequited love and hanging out with people who didn't share my enthusiasm for the socio-political movements of the era. I was in a rut of goofing off and having fun times, but little else. My prior antiwar activism had been on hold for the most part since the murders at Kent State and Jackson State. Those killings had a chilling effect on many young people. And wasn't that the intention...to shoot young American students to stifle dissent? I wanted to assert myself again, but wasn't sure how to do it.

The war in Vietnam was still raging without an end in sight. In 1969, I was among those men whose fate was determined by the circus sideshow event called "the first draft lottery." It was televised on TV, just like "The Price Is Right". Two cages with turners, one containing numbers 1 - 366, the other with individual cubes containing the month and day of the month, were spun, and each individual day was matched to a number. The birth dates matched to the lower numbers meant that men born on that date would be among the first to be drafted.

Fortunately for me, a high number was drawn for my birth date which meant that I would never be selected for active duty. However, I felt an obligation to help those fighting the war against their wishes. Richard Nixon expanded the war into Southeast Asia which caused the deaths of many people on both sides. Nixon had to be stopped in 1972. That's when politics called my name.

One year earlier, I played a minor role on campus during the "Joe Duffey for Senate" campaign. Rev. Duffy was the Democratic candidate for the US Senate seat in 1970. He had been a supporter of Eugene McCarthy's presidential campaign in 1968 and was head of the antiwar group "Americans for Democratic Action." I helped other students set up the room in which Duffey gave a speech at Western Connecticut State University. Ultimately, he lost the election to Lowell Weicker, but my brief foray into the world of politics within the Duffey campaign made me want to do more.

In the autumn of 1971, I heard about a Senator from South Dakota who was against the Vietnam War and vowed to end it if he became the next president. His name was George McGovern. I answered an ad in the college newspaper about his candidacy and became the student coordinator for the McGovern campaign at WestConn. Also, I joined the college's Young Democrats organization. One of the WestConn Young Democrats was a very passionate political student by the name of Jim Dyer. Several years later, Jim was elected mayor of Danbury. Now deceased, Mayor Dyer served in that capacity through the late 80s. He was always very kind and helpful to me, and like many present day Danbury residents, I will never forget him.

I had very little experience in campaigning. Thankfully, I received assistance and advice from those at the statewide "McGovern for President" headquarters in New Haven. The 1972 presidential election was the first one in which 18-20 year olds could vote. My first goal was to get McGovern's name known among the young student body. Daily, I handed out brochures and campaign position papers at the student union snack bar. Eventually, I received permission to set up a table near the campus book store....a great location as many students passed by all day. I couldn't have done it without help from George Macri, a fellow student who was in many of my history classes. George had some prior experience with political campaigning in his hometown of Meriden CT. Together, the two of us tackled the most important objective of the McGovern campaign at that time...recruiting volunteers to work on behalf of the candidate in the upcoming New Hampshire presidential primary in March.

We had sign-up sheets for weekend trips to New Hampshire. Several people volunteered to make the trip to the snowy Granite State and go door to door canvassing and talking up Senator McGovern to potential Democratic primary voters. The first time I went was by a bus chartered from

Fairfield University. We spent the weekend campaigning in Portsmouth. When we returned to the WestConn campus, a few more names were on our sign-up list, including several women who lived in the Litchfield Dormitory. The weekend before the crucial primary, George, two "dormies" named Vicki and Donna, another guy named Phil, and I loaded into George's VW microbus and headed for the University of New Hampshire in Durham.

It was late at night by the time we reached our destination. When we arrived at McGovern headquarters, they gave us the name of a local Catholic Church providing lodging for volunteers. We stepped over bodies in sleeping bags in a room downstairs and were guided to the inside of the church. Dog tired, we unrolled our sleeping bags behind the last pew. I tucked myself in for the night while two guys smoked a joint in the confessional. A huge crucifix stared at me as I drifted off to sleep. The next day, we were referred to a family of McGovern supporters who allowed us the run of their home over the next few days. We reported back to headquarters and took our instructions from them, including canvassing potential voters and poll-watching on the day of the primary.

The trip wasn't all work. One night we went to a huge fundraiser attended by McGovern himself. We met him briefly and shook hands with the senator. In my zeal, I rushed through an auditorium door not looking where I was going and elbowed a man hard in his stomach. My eyes met the startled visage of Pierre Salinger, who held his tongue, but appeared to be quite angry at me...I mumbled an apology. The former JFK press secretary wasn't the only well-known person we met during our visit to New Hampshire. On a dare from Vicki, I walked up to actor Paul Newman, who was campaigning for Republican antiwar candidate, Pete McCloskey (Congressman from California), in his quixotic attempt to beat Nixon in the Republican primary. I was a fan of Newman. We talked about McGovern for a few minutes. He did have those bold blue eyes, but they were quite bloodshot that day.

Although McGovern did well in the primary, he lost to Senator Ed Muskie from Maine. We were a bit discouraged over the loss, but encouraged that Senator McGovern had increased his popularity for the rest of the primary season. For me, the lasting benefit from the New Hampshire primary was a romantic one. By the time our trip was over, and we were back in CT, Donna and I become a couple. If it hadn't been for the McGovern campaign, we would never have met. Over 40 years later, we are still together.

After the disastrous and violent 1968 Democratic Convention in Chicago, a commission was set up to establish new rules for state Democratic parties to select delegates. Ironically the commission was headed by Senator McGovern, who resigned from it when he announced his candidacy for president in 1971. The new rules loosened up the state delegation process leading to more democracy in selection and diversity of delegates...women and minority groups had to be taken into consideration. Many states decided to have primaries to select delegates for the National convention, replacing the traditional party-boss controlled conventions of the past.

These new rules filtered down to city and town levels as well. Danbury was no exception. The Democratic Town

Committee was responsible for picking candidates. In 1972, the members of the Town committee were centrist and conservative, not willing to promote and select delegates for candidates like George McGovern or any candidate left of center. A group of liberal Democrats, dedicated to social justice, mounted a challenge to the Town Committee members by forcing an election and running its own slate of candidates. The liberals ran nine of their own candidates. I was one of them.

At age 21, I joined eight other Danbury Democrats in an attempt to unseat some of the people who occupied the Town committee. Among my fellow challengers was William (Bill) Goodman. He and his wife June were long time Danbury political activists. They knew my name because of my involvement in the McGovern campaign and from my many letters-to-the-editor in the Danbury News-Times. I was flattered when they asked me to join the diverse group of nine candidates (consisting also of women and minorities), but I was also a bit apprehensive about plunging into the uncharted waters of running for office.

Using the canvassing skills I acquired while working in the New Hampshire primary, I walked up and down the streets of my neighborhood on Danbury's Southside. Some folks invited me into their homes to speak at length about why I wanted their vote, while others listened politely for a few minutes. Donna helped me in my efforts by making phone calls on my behalf. Then the big day of the election came. It was strange to see my name listed as a candidate inside the voting machine at South Street School, the same school where I attended kindergarten through 6th Grade. However, when the day was over and all the votes were counted, we lost...all nine of us. None of the sitting Town Committee members were replaced, but our voices had been heard. Over the next few years, reform came to Democratic politics in Danbury, the rest of Connecticut and the nation.

In November 1972, as yet unscathed by the Watergate break-in five months earlier, Richard Nixon defeated George McGovern with ease. The Democratic National Committee didn't helped McGovern as much as it could have during the campaign. They failed (or didn't try very hard) to get Nixon to debate him. They left the senator to dangle in the wind. Tricky Dick Nixon was still in charge of the nation. It was a discouraging time to say the least.

I was a recent college graduate, 22 years old, engaged to be married, but unemployed. Politics took a back seat to my personal life in 1973.

CHAPTER TWENTY-FOUR---Go East Young Man

Back in high school during the late 1960s, our guidance counselors told us that we would be successful if we studied hard, did well on our SATs and received B.A. degrees, but by the time we graduated from college that was not the case. Instead, during the early-to-mid 1970s the Sixties Generation encountered inflation caused by war spending and an oil shortage crisis started by the Arab nations. The latter was exploited by the greed of American oil companies. Jobs were scarce...at least those that people had been trained to do. Also, the first indication that computers would become the focus of future work appeared on the horizon. Many young people were prepared for the Liberal Arts occupations their teachers promised them, but not for the reality of data entry positions.

By the beginning of 1973, I had no job. However, that didn't stop my fiancée, Donna, and I from setting a wedding date in September. A couple of months into the year, I took a Federal Government civil service exam and scored very well. Less than a month later, I received a letter requesting me to attend a panel interview for a Service Representative position with the Social Security Administration (SSA). My father drove me to the Federal Building in Bridgeport where I sat with several other prospective candidates. We were interviewed by a panel of district managers from SSA offices in the area, including New Haven, Stamford, and Bridgeport. We were told that SSA was hiring employees nationwide to assist with a new Federal income program called Supplemental Security Income (SSI). After a series of questions, mostly concerning how we would handle awkward situations with customers and supervisors, the interviewers thanked us and said that letters would be sent to us about our job status.

Not long afterwards, I received official word that I had been hired as a Service Representative. I was assigned to the SSA district office in Stamford. There were several dozen new employees hired statewide. All of us attended a six week training class at the Federal Building in Hartford. I stayed at a nearby hotel. For most of my training in May and June of 1973, it was class during the day and watching the Watergate hearings in the evening.

I bought a 1973 Dodge Colt, pastel yellow in color, for $2700. My future father-in-law, Art DiRienzo, said I paid too much, but it was a sturdy car that lasted 11 years, went through two major accidents, made two round trips across the continent, and drove through the White Desert without air conditioning...finally succumbing to a road ice accident in 1984.

Donna and I were married in her hometown of Branford CT on September 22, 1973. We rented an apartment on Belltown Road in Stamford. Most weekends we visited our parents...mine in Danbury, Donna's family in Branford. As we grew more accustomed to Stamford, we spent more time there. We developed new friendships, especially with my coworkers, Lorraine Esposito, her husband Paul, and Steve Leshin. I worked 17 years for Social Security. The job paid well, but I never liked it.

There was an "Us vs. Them" philosophy which pervaded the thinking of upper management in our relations with the customers. We were told to get the public in and out of the office as quickly as possible so processing times would look good on our weekly statistics. On one occasion, I was assigned for a week to the branch office in Norwalk. It was there that the branch manager yelled at me for "taking too long" when I interviewed a sobbing woman whose husband had died the previous day. Should I have said, "C'mon lady, your husband will be dead forever, but I don't have all day," as I glanced at my watch?

Also, I was disillusioned with the SSI program which had been a State assistance program and then handed over to the Federal government in early 1974. The hoops and barrels placed in the way of poor and disabled people trying to obtain benefits were often dehumanizing and unfair. The proofs employees had to obtain, and the payment calculations we had to make, were confusing. As unhappy as the job made me, I was thankful for the lifelong friendships I made while working for SSA (many of which have lasted four decades and counting). It was the best part of working for Social Security.

Towards the end of 1973, the "Arab Oil Embargo" was in place. Gas stations rationed gasoline, even though tankers with fuel sat off shore and domestic oil reserves were not used. Our apartment was right next to a gas station on the corner of Belltown Rd and Burdick Rd. At the end of each week, we woke up at 5 AM to get in line and hope there would still be gas available when we reached the pump.

Nixon was still president, but not for long. The date was Friday, August 9, 1974. My friend and coworker, Steve Leshin, walked into the reception area of our SSA office and removed Nixon's presidential portrait from the wall. Only a few minutes earlier, Nixon announced his resignation. Upon hearing the news, Steve knew he had a public service to perform. As he removed the photo of the man with the beady eyes and phony smile, customers in the reception area broke into spontaneous cheers and applause.

After a year of living in Stamford, which is part of the major metropolitan New York City area, I wanted to get away from the crowds and manic traffic. I saw a TV program about living in Arizona. The state seemed so free, wide open and tranquil. I wrote away to an office in Phoenix and received information about the many cities and regions in Arizona. Donna and I decided to take a vacation there in August 1974.

Prescott AZ stood out as a possible destination to reside. The literature I received made it seem ideal. The city was one mile in elevation with pine-coned forests, mountains, mild winters, and a big town square. Phoenix was only a two hour drive to the south and Flagstaff two hours to the north. On our trip, we saw the Grand Canyon, the ghost town of Jerome, Oak Creek Canyon and the palm trees of Phoenix, but Prescott beckoned us. While there, I dropped into the local SSA office, had a conversation with the District Manager, and talked about relocating to their office. However, the Prescott office didn't have a Service Rep position available at the time. The manager shook my hand and said "we'll keep you in mind."

When we arrived back home in Stamford, the first thing I did was call my parents to let them know that we were OK. My sister answered the phone and I regaled her with stories about our experiences in the Grand Canyon State. I was so excited telling her about our trip that I failed to notice how quiet she was. When I stopped to take a breath, she told me the bad news...Grandma Bella died while I was away. Instantly, I was overcome with grief...going from a high to a low in a matter of seconds. My grandmother meant so much to me. Every year while I was growing up, she stayed with us for a couple of weeks during the summer to get away from her small apartment in Manhattan and also visited for a week or so during the holiday season in December. In between we went to the city to visit her. However, her health had been deteriorating over the last couple of years. A stroke had taken its toll on her in 1973. And now she was gone. According to Jewish custom and religious rules, burials must take place by sunset of the day following the day of death. Grandma's funeral was over and done while we were in Arizona. In an era before cell phones and computers, my parents didn't know where to call us while we were traveling.

A few weeks after our vacation, I received a phone call on the inter-office government line at work. The voice on the other end belonged to the manager from the Prescott AZ office. He told me there was a Service Rep opening in their office and it was mine if I wanted it. However, I had to give them my decision in three days. It was a life-altering decision for both Donna and me to make. We also had to take into account how such a transcontinental move might affect our parents. After a couple of days, our decision was made. On to Arizona we went.

Donna and I lived in Prescott AZ from 1974 to 1977. It was a radical change from the New England towns we knew since childhood. We were all alone when we arrived and had to fend for ourselves. The experience was like being away in the military for three years, but without having to endure boot camp. Back then, Prescott was a small city with two grocery stores, a "Jack-in-the-Box" fast food hamburger joint, and "34 Flavors" and "Harlan's" (Western talk for "Baskin-Robbins" and "Kentucky Fried Chicken" respectively). There wasn't much selection at the "Fry's" grocery store. Italian or Chinese food was almost nonexistent...we could only find it two hours down the road in Phoenix.

Similar to New England in one respect, the center of the city contained the county court house in the middle of a large tree lined public square. The pace of life in Prescott was slower than in CT. People looked each other in the eye and said hello when you walked past them, instead of the furtive glance and quick look-away prevalent in big cities on the East coast. Donna and I lost our New England accents forever while we were there. We bought our first home on Robinson Drive. Whenever there were household fix-it problems, we asked for advice from my coworker, Lupe Enriquez and her husband, Roberto. The biggest event of the year in Prescott was the annual rodeo (claimed to be the oldest of its kind in the nation) and frontier days during the 4th of July holiday week. Tourists flocked to the city. Everyone who walked the town square had to wear at least two articles of Western clothing or risk being placed in the makeshift jail until someone paid the charity-based "bail". Donna and I bought boots and cowboy hats for the occasion.

During our time in Arizona, we became lifelong friends with fellow SSA workers Chuck Curradi and Steve Meltzer and Steve's wife, Liz Doup. We spent a memorable Bicentennial 4th of July with Steve and Liz in San Diego, where we were greeted at the gates of that city's famous Zoo by a Hare Krishna devotee wearing an Uncle Sam outfit as he distributed copies of the Bhagavad Gita....an image impossible to forget. While living in Prescott, I became aware of the plight and discrimination of Indians and Mexican-Americans. On my own, I studied socialism, the writings of Malcolm X, and couldn't stop reading a book called "Roots." It was the beginning of many years of self-taught post-college education.

As beautiful as Prescott was with its bright sunsets, brilliant rainbows, and the snow-capped Humphreys Peak that we could see from our back porch, I became restless. I wanted to be doing something else instead of the SSA job which I found unfulfilling on several levels. I was promoted to a Claims Representative position in 1975, but despite a step up on the pay scale, all SSA offices were the same no matter where in the country one worked...kind of like working at McDonald's (show me your birth certificate...would you like fries with that, sir?). I could transfer to almost anywhere in the USA, but would continue to work at a job I didn't like. Still, that didn't deter me from trying one more time to move a great distance in an attempt to leave SSA...or not.

There are times in one's life when a greater force takes over and you do things that you don't understand. That's what happened to me in the late spring of 1977. My mind was guided by a higher power. All of a sudden my main thrust in life was to move away from AZ and return back East. To this day, I remember the superficial rationale...to move where I might get a job writing for a living and to be closer to my aging parents. But, that wasn't the reason, although that's what I told everyone. As we packed up all of our belongings and drove east across the continent, I kept asking myself, "Why am I doing this?" But, it was out of my control. I had to let it happen.

We moved back East, but not to Connecticut. Instead I transferred to the SSA office in Ithaca NY, several hours away from the New York City rat race. This time we went to a place where we knew someone, my Aunt Ruth and Uncle Sid. It didn't take us long to become acclimated to our surroundings. I made friends easily at the SSA office and was able to tolerate the job most of the time. Also, just within a few weeks of my arrival in the Finger Lakes, I had two record reviews published in the weekly alternative newspaper, the Ithaca Times. One was about the "Heroes" album by David Bowie, the other a new live album by the Rolling Stones. I couldn't believe my good fortune. In a few weeks, I accomplished more in terms of being published than in all the previous years combined.

Ithaca was ideal for people our age and a bit older. It was a haven for those who espoused Sixties beliefs in freedom and equality. There were communes, collective farming and markets, book stores, weekly newspapers, an alternative "hippie" bank, yoga and meditation retreats, new age practitioners, acupuncturists, ultra-liberal politicians...they even printed their own local money.

I still don't understand why we moved to Ithaca, but it's where we were meant to be.

CHAPTER TWENTY FIVE---You May Say I'm A Dreamer

In the late 1970s, I wrote a weekly music column for the Ithaca Times. They wanted me to interview local bands. The articles I did were acceptable, but contained little enthusiasm (the groups were musically uninteresting for the most part). One day, the editor dumped me, matter-of-factly, as we stood together in the check-out line at the CVS pharmacy on the Ithaca Commons. Although I didn't think so at the time, it was for the better. I never would have made it as a journalist. I tend not to write well unless the subject is one that excites me or involves me on a personal level. Shortly after my column ended, a new writing idea hit me. I *had* to do it.

My friend, Paul Esposito, was working on a doctoral thesis in Sociology. To accomplish his goal, Paul advertised for letters from people asking them to detail their experiences regarding his particular research subject. It dawned on me that this methodology could be used in writing about popular culture. It had been almost ten years since The Beatles broke up. I was quite discouraged with the disco laden songs of the late 70s. I began to wonder whether people, other than me, remembered the Fab Four and if the band continued to influence them. Borrowing from Paul Esposito's idea, I began to advertise in several magazines and newspapers for responses from people whose lives were affected by The Beatles. I received many. The largest quantity of letters and essays came from ads I placed in Rolling Stone magazine in 1979 and 1980. All together, I received over 200 letters and fan artwork. Then, I had to figure out what to do with them all.

There were definite themes and personality types revealed in the letters. Some of the writers were people who became musicians because of The Beatles, women whose ideal mates were based on the individual characteristics of John, Paul, George and Ringo, folks who chose careers because of The Beatles positive and peaceful influence, and younger fans born during the Sixties, who discovered the band after the break-up. The letters and essays I received were a breath of fresh air. Many people carried the spirit of the Sixties in their hearts which influenced their lives in a multitude of ways from the personal to the political. I assembled the letters into thematic chapters, adding my own two cents along the way, and began to organize them into a manuscript typed on a brand new Smith-Corona electric typewriter that I bought for the occasion.

It was 1980. I worked on the book despite encountering physical problems due to a deteriorated disc in my neck. This painful condition led to many trips for physical therapy. Additionally, a very pesky stomach ailment made me wonder why these things were happening to me before I was 30 years old. And then that summer, age 30 happened to me. I never believed in the expression, "don't trust anyone over 30", made popular during the Berkeley Free Speech movement in 1965. However, I was wary of attaining age 30. In fact, I was downright depressed by it. To my mind, age 30 signified the end of youth and was also a painful acknowledgement that I hadn't accomplished more in my life. I wanted to stop being a claims representative for the Social Security Administration and become a published book author, but failed at both.

Donna and I spent my 30th birthday driving from my in-laws' home in Connecticut to my parents' apartment in Maine as Hurricane Charley chased us north on I-95. The storm loomed as a gloomy presence in the rear view mirror of our brown Mazda wagon. The hurricane's darkness matched my disposition.

A couple of weeks later, well established in my "old age", some news arrived that buoyed my spirits. John Lennon was coming out of his self-imposed exile from the music world. After 5 years, John Lennon and Yoko Ono were about to make a new album. Two years earlier, I missed a chance to meet the Lennons. A man I knew in Arizona began a magazine and published one of my articles. Somehow, he made inroads to one of John and Yoko's assistants and began to negotiate permission to interview the famous couple. The guy from AZ was going to fly to New York to interview John and Yoko and I planned on joining him as the photographer. The article was scheduled to appear in a future issue of the new magazine. However, the plans fell through because the Lennons were not ready to be interviewed. Discouraged, yes, but having that close call helped me focus more on the idea of finishing the chapters of my book.

I was approaching the home stretch of putting together the book, "As I Write This Letter: An American Generation Remembers The Beatles", when I took a break to do a different writing assignment. A local Ithaca restaurant owner, Michael Turback, started a New York City based publication called "Bedroom Magazine". The magazine was designed with couples in mind, so I pitched a writing idea to Michael about John and Yoko. He was aware that the Lennons were back in the news and agreed to my proposal. I submitted the article to Turback in October and it was all set to be printed during the second week of December.

In the 1960s, my aunt and uncle, Ruth and Sid Mesibov, lived at 41 West 72nd St in Manhattan. It was fun to leave my home in Danbury to visit them, stroll in nearby Central Park, and walk to the Museum of Natural History. However, it was a scary route as well. On the corner of W. 72nd St and Central Park West, there was a foreboding building surrounded by wrought-iron railings with gargoyles. I walked by quickly, not wanting to look at the images. That building was called the Dakota. I learned from Aunt Ruth that many well known writers, actors, and other celebrities lived there. I saw a gate where cars drove through to a man sitting in a gold colored booth. Cheerfully, he allowed access to the famous tenants of the apartment house. Back then, I never guessed the Dakota would one day be the home of John and Yoko Lennon.

During late 1980, John Lennon was written about in Newsweek, Rolling Stone, and the New York Times. For a man who had been absent from the public eye for several years, Lennon was being talked about everywhere. The album, "Double Fantasy" was released around Thanksgiving. It had been years since John issued an album of original material. He sounded older and wiser, but still hip and relevant with "Woman" and "Watching The Wheels". There was talk of John and Yoko releasing a follow-up album and going on tour in early 1981.

Excitement was in the air...a dream come true for fans...a dream that became a nightmare.

There was nothing unusual about December 8, 1980. It was a typical Monday work day. I ate dinner, watched M*A*S*H, and went to bed around 10:30. Around midnight, a nerve-jangling phone call startled me from sleep. Donna answered it. I could hear her speaking quickly in a surprised voice. She handed the phone to me and said it was our Arizona friend, Steve Meltzer. Then she told me,

"John Lennon was killed."

Sometimes, the brain works faster than we expect. Several thoughts can race through the mind in a twinkling of a few seconds. Immediately, the images of a car or airplane crash popped into my head. That must be what happened, I thought, but then Steve said to me,

"Some guy just walked up to John and shot him."

My mindset was so sure that John had died in an accident...nothing prepared me for the horrible raw reality of someone shooting him. I was in shock. I stumbled around my house in desperation...searching for what...I don't know. I turned on the TV, but at that late hour in 1980 there were no stations broadcasting live news on my cable service. But what if Steve was wrong...yeah that had to be it...maybe it was just a rumor. So, I turned on the radio. As I moved the dial from one station to another, each was playing a Beatles or Lennon song...that's when it hit me...that's when I knew...John Lennon was dead. Pacing in the hallway, I cried out, "I'm never gonna be the same", realizing instantly the truth of that prediction.

Naively perhaps, I expected that many people I knew from the Ithaca area would feel my level of grief. However, in the immediate aftermath of John Lennon's death, and during the next few years that followed, I was often the recipient of unsympathetic responses from some of my friends and acquaintances. They could not understand why I was upset over the murder of a man who I didn't know personally and hadn't known me. "After all Marc," they said, "It's not like he was a relative."

But, they were wrong.

Lennon, ten years older than me, was the big brother I never had. As a teenager, I wanted a big brother who had experienced the ups and downs of growing up and could offer advice as I went through my high school years. I didn't want an older brother to live my life for me, but someone who would listen to my problems, provide words of encouragement and not be afraid to provide a "reality check" if necessary. Lennon provided that guidance for me in song, words and actions during the Sixties. After the phone call informing me of his death, I felt like a little kid whose big brother was killed in a war and would never come home again.

The rest of that week after December 8th was extremely difficult. I tried to return to normal, went back to work, but felt numb most of the time. At one point, in a fit of anger and grief, I took down all the Beatles and Lennon posters from the walls in my study. What was the point of looking at them anymore? How could it possibly have any meaning now? Within the next couple of hours, I regretted my impulsiveness and placed all of the photos and posters back where they belonged. However, I couldn't stand hearing any Beatles or Lennon music, especially the "Double Fantasy" album I listened to daily for the past couple of weeks. "Beautiful Boy", the song that John wrote about his son, was unbearable now. Everything sounded like a dirge. My nerves were close to the surface. Up until December 8th, the words "Death" and "Beatles" had nothing in common.

Yoko Ono asked the world to remember John by observing ten minutes of silence at 2:00 PM EST on Sunday, December 14th, six days after his death. People all over the globe, most notably in New York and Liverpool, gathered in the thousands to honor her request. Many others participated privately or in small groups. Hundreds of radio stations, particularly those that played Beatles and Lennon songs, went off the air for ten minutes, a tribute never done before or since. I observed the ten minutes of silence while sitting in my study. I had my favorite local FM Rock station on. It was eerie to hear the music stop, so I checked other stations for a few seconds...they also were off the air. I prayed, sobbed and said good-bye. Then, the 10 minutes of silence was over...and what passed for reality set in.

Today, I am more than twice the age I was in 1980. During the first few years after John Lennon's death, I was often sad...part of me died that night too. By the late 80s, I had enough of grief and began to celebrate Lennon instead of mourn for him. No doubt, I still missed John's keen insight on different issues, but the joy and wonder of his songs and lyrics outweighed the shock and negativity of his death. The emptiness inside of me was starting to heal. Once I let go of the impossible quest to understand why he was killed, I was able to concentrate on his legacy and its positive effects. John Lennon was a musical and lyrical genius...a guide for an entire generation...but in death he has become more of an "Everyman" than an icon, representing all the attributes and flaws any of us have.

I realize that "Everyman" aspect of John Lennon each time I visit the Strawberry Fields section of Central Park and witness a cross-section of society gazing upon the memorial to him. Embedded in the sidewalk next to the 72nd Street entrance is a circular mosaic of black and white tiles in an interlocking design. The word, IMAGINE, sits inside a circle in the middle. People gather around, usually speaking quietly to one another, as they look, remember, and pay their respects, often leaving flowers on the tiles.

A recurring theme began in John's life and music during the early 1970s. He thought that peace could only be achieved through non-violence and spread by one person to another. This concept showed up in his minimalist approach to his songs. Far from being utopian or naïve, as some would claim, the lyrics to "Imagine" gave simple instructions for contemplating the future, similar to the famous Gandhi quote, "be the change you want to see in the world".

The black and white contrast in the mosaic in Central Park captures the duality of John Lennon, a complex man and a minimalist, whose words and music represent hope. By his life's end, Lennon kept his focus. He never wanted to be a leader even though many saw him as one. In 1980, John reminded us that, individually and together, we had the ability to achieve peace and love on our own.

John Lennon was not someone to be placed on a pedestal or revered as a martyr. John was one of us. As I wrote in my book, "As I Write This Letter",

"We knew he put his pants on one leg at a time because we saw him with his pants off."

EPILOGUE--After The Sixties

The political and cultural decade known as the Sixties ended around 1973/1974, but for me the Sixties were really over in 1980 with the election of Ronald Reagan and the assassination of John Lennon. It was the advent of a darker age...mourning in America...a corporate takeover. As in the cartoon "Yellow Submarine," the Blue Meanies sucked all of the color from the world.

When I look back in time, there is a black wedge stuck at the end of 1980. It's a marker, a before and after designation. In addition to the loss of John Lennon (the man), his death symbolized the end of a joyful resistance. The tide of radical conservatism in the form of Reaganism seemed unstoppable.

There is a phrase popular in liberal circles, "it all began with Reagan." The phrase fixes blame for all the chaos, economic inequality and overt racism prevalent in the USA today on Ronald Reagan. It's a simplistic explanation...but damn if it isn't true. Greed and avarice received a gigantic push with the election of Ronald Reagan. His regime transformed the United States away from democracy and freedom to the near corporate oligarchy we live in today. They took their cue from the Business Roundtable's demand for a merger of business and politics, while the Lewis Powell Memo (authored by the future Supreme Court Justice) provided a blueprint for business to "take back" the nation and gave corporations permission to gain a dominant political foothold in America. The conservative government takeover required no coup as it appealed to many voters' baser instincts. Ultimately, Reaganism resulted in the economic depression of 2008 and the near destruction of America's middle class.

Corporate America began to dominate the media during the early 1980s. The ownership of newspapers, magazines, radio stations, and TV networks fell into the hands of Big Business which had no previous ties to mass media. The danger of this concentrated power over the news we see and hear was outlined by the late Ben Bagdikian in his book, "The Media Monopoly" (1983). Bagdikian's alarming predictions about the effect of a few conglomerates controlling the distribution of information have all come true. The "dumbing down" of America began in the early 1980s. USA Today and People Magazine led the way.

This was a far cry from the past when newspapers, radio, and TV were owned independently by families and small syndicates. Back in the day, news divisions on TV were operated separately from entertainment departments. Although sponsors and advertisers exerted pressure and censorship, news was news...there was very little fluff or entertainment disguised as such. If man bit dog, journalists tried to find out why. Antiwar demonstrations, though not commented upon favorably, were covered on the news. So were civil rights marches and other progressive movements. Those events may not have been covered in depth, but they occupied a good portion of the nightly news and were often above the fold in newspapers. That ended with the corporate domination of the news. They didn't give coverage to those they perceived as enemies of the bottom line.

During the Sixties, youth questioning authority, economic inequality, and championing freedom and democracy caused

Corporate America to shake in their boots. It was unexpected. They didn't know what hit them. At first, they resorted to ridicule and hoped it would go away. However, once the Corporatists bought and controlled the media, the reactionaries pushed back harder. The revisionism of Sixties history began.

In this new history, the conservative news shapers portrayed the Sixties Generation as a paradox by vilifying them for protesting against the Vietnam war and questioning authority while criticizing the same generation for not doing more in those endeavors. First, we were blamed for starting a revolution and then we were accused of not seeing it through. In reality, it was the policies and legislation enacted by corporate funded politicians that exacerbated poverty, the environment, and increased unemployment, but it was much easier to blame all those kids with their long hair, Rock music, and belief in equality. It was a lot easier to destroy the economic progress made by the middle class, who had enabled their children to afford college, than it was to expand educational opportunities for all.

What became known as the "Culture Wars" became widespread in the 1980s when Corporate American jumped into bed with the Radical Right and Fundamentalist Christians. George Bush, Reagan's successor, was quite successful in destroying the "Vietnam Syndrome" (the reluctance to engage in battle after the Vietnam War) when he led troops to the Persian Gulf in 1991. The chants of "USA USA USA" from jingoistic Cornell frat boys on the Ithaca Commons still ring in my ears.

There are some people who say that the Sixties Generation sold out during the late 70s and early 80s. They accuse them of not caring about war and peace once the war in Vietnam was over. These folks contend that Sixties Gen gave up on its values of fairness and equality and then became cut-throat business people caring only about profits and little about the poor. I don't believe that at all.

When the Sixties ended, there was a unity of opinion on what was wrong with the United States and what needed to be done to fix it. However, there was no unity of numbers...no organizations existed to carry people from an antiwar footing into practice. Corporate America, as noted previously, took advantage of that situation and retaliated in overkill against the ideals and foundations of a generation, often using economic tactics (oil embargo, inflation) to try and slow down the momentum. However, the overlooked story about the Sixties Generation in the 70s and 80s is the influence they had upon the nation as a whole. No matter where they settled, things went from "walking the walk to talking the talk" within individual towns, counties and states. Many members of Sixties Gen became teachers, planners, economists, school board members, local politicians and organizers of non-profit advocacy groups who introduced progressive programs across the United States. They weren't flashy...there were no headlines in the corporate controlled media...but their impact was felt at the grass roots level. "Think globally and act locally" became a reality.

As for me, I got older and some of my priorities changed. Hell...life changed. I wrote. I tried to sell articles about music. I was published for awhile as a local music critic. I wrote a book about The Beatles which was published by a small press.

I attended a million persons anti-nuke demonstration in the streets of Manhattan and smaller rallies at the Seneca Army Depot in Romulus NY. I marched against Ronald Reagan's war against labor unions at the gigantic Solidarity Day rally in Washington DC (Donna with me at each event). I railed against the use of Beatles music in TV commercials and started my own organization to combat it. Often, I was a one-man opinion writer against those who tried to portray the Vietnam War as a "noble effort."

In 1986, Donna and I adopted a baby girl from Korea. I quit working for Social Security in 1989. Then, in 1990, I came face-to-face with a diagnosis of cancer. Thankfully, the medical advances of the time saved me. I survived. However, that survival made me question what my life was all about. In the early 1990s, I dropped out of the 20th century rat race, discovered myself, and then opened a used book store. Economically, my family had hardships due to my scant income, but I was able to open my eyes, mind, and heart to my spiritual side...something that had been dormant for a couple of decades. I began to meditate. I read dozens of self-help books, then New Age books. I disbelieved less. I had other worldly experiences. It was as if a self-protective barrier was shed and a receptive being named "Marc" emerged.

I began to grow my hair long again for the first time since the 70s. I explored different possibilities of earning a buck. I wrote a book which was eventually published as "The Giant's Chair." Unfortunately, my book store, Second Chance Books, was a financial disaster and closed in 1996. However, I read and studied so much literature about religion and mysticism that it was the equivalent of earning a post-grad degree. And when it came time for me to re-enter the work world, I was hired by an organization dedicated to recycling used materials and eliminating waste by re-use.

When I look back at my life so far and the Sixties Generation as a whole, I see an amazing journey unfold. 50 years ago, an entire generation was on the same wavelength, receiving the same signal on individual antennae. As time went on, we took different paths, imparting and receiving knowledge along the way, but age isn't going to stop us from going forward.

There will come a time when the birds stop chirping, but not until our song is over.

The End?

About the Author

Marc Catone writes frequently about the cultural and political events of the Sixties. His first book, *As I Write This Letter: An American Generation Remembers The Beatles*, contains fan letters, essays and artwork about The Beatles. It was published in 1982. His second book, *The Giant's Chair*, a Sixties tale about lost faith and redemption, was released in 2005. Both are available at Amazon. There is also a Kindle version of *The Giant's Chair*. Other essays and articles by Marc have appeared in Beatlefan magazine, the Danbury News-Times, and the Ithaca Journal as well as the online publications, CounterPunch and CommonDreams.

Marc has worked for various employers over the years, most notably for one of the most progressive recycling and reuse centers in the nation, Tompkins County Solid Waste Management, located in Ithaca NY. Now retired, Marc intends to continue his writings and try to keep up with his grandchildren. Visit his website:

http://marccatone.webs.com